FROM THE ROYAL FLYING CORPS
TO THE RACE TO CIRCUMNAVIGATE
THE GLOBE

FROM THE ROYAL FLYING CORPS TO THE RACE TO CIRCUMNAVIGATE THE GLOBE

THE ADVENTURES OF SQUADRON LEADER

ARCHIBALD STUART-MACLAREN

VANESSA ASCOUGH

FONTHILL

First published in Great Britain in 2026 by
Fonthill
An imprint of
Pen & Sword Books Ltd
Yorkshire – Philadelphia

A CIP catalogue record for this book
is available from the British Library.

Typeset in SabonLTStd 11/15 by
SJmagic DESIGN SERVICES, India.
Printed and bound in the UK by CPI Group (UK) Ltd, Croydon, CR0 4YY

The Publisher's authorised representative in the EU for product
safety is Authorised Rep Compliance Ltd., Ground Floor,
71 Lower Baggot Street, Dublin D02 P593, Ireland.
www.arccompliance.com

For a complete list of Pen & Sword titles please contact

PEN & SWORD BOOKS LIMITED
George House, Units 12 & 13, Beevor Street, Off Pontefract Road,
Barnsley, South Yorkshire, S71 1HN, England
E-mail: enquiries@pen-and-sword.co.uk
Website: www.pen-and-sword.co.uk

or

PEN AND SWORD BOOKS
1950 Lawrence Rd, Havertown, PA 19083, USA
E-mail: uspen-and-sword@casematepublishers.com
Website: www.penandswordbooks.com

Biography can reveal what a society cares about, what it values. By encountering the values of another person in another time we can learn more about our own.

—Kate Kirkpatrick, *Becoming Beauvoir* (Bloomsbury, 2019)

Consider the known and unknown generations of your family. They have given you the foundations of your spirit.

—credo of James Mackean Evers

Acknowledgements

Since I began my research into my grandfather's life, I have had the most astounding fortune to meet and make contact with many people who have contributed to my understanding of who he was and what he achieved.

I am so grateful to the late John Washington-Smith for introducing me to the families of Plenderleith and Andrews—the crew of the World Flight. Andrew's son, Charles, so very kindly gave me his original written account of the World Flight, and I could not have acquired as much knowledge as I have without it. Many of the original photographs have come from the Plenderleith family album. Also, my grandfather's brother, Cecil, followed the World Flight in much detail and collected a great deal of newspaper cuttings and photographs all along the way, although many of them are undated.

I would like to thank all the people who found me online, got in touch and sent photographs and wonderful archival material. These include the archivists at the National Archives in Kew, Army Flying Museum, Royal Air Force Museum, Air Historical Branch (RAF), National Museum of the Royal Navy, Brooklands Museum Trust, Fleet Air Arm Museum, Forces War Records, Shell Historical Heritage and Archive, Editor of *Flight Magazine*, Summer Fields School, Wellington College and Eton College.

So much help and information were given to me from Cross and Cockade International, the author Michael Napier and those who sent me photographs from their grandfather's and great grandfather's collections, including Adrian Bower and the grandson of Captain

Blackburn. There was also a gentleman in Benderlock, Scotland who discovered an atlas in his late mother's attic which had original writings by my grandfather in it about the World Flight, which he kindly sent to me.

When I attended the T. E. Lawrence Symposium in Southampton I was so lucky to meet up with the grandson of Air Chief Marshal Sir Geoffrey Salmond, who my grandfather knew well and flew with over the years. Also, I received a good deal of help from those who gave talks on that day.

My connection with Canada has proved to be invaluable, and my thanks go to all those who spent so much time doing research for me as well as inviting me to give talks and presentations on the World Flight.

The way the book looks and the inspiration behind its layout rests with my literary designer Steve Hogan, my original editor and proofreader Marcus Parry and my amazing husband Roger, who has contributed a great deal of wonderful thoughts and ideas over the years and never stopped encouraging me to be as adventurous as I can be.

Finally, a true understanding of my grandfather's personality came from the many little stories my late mother, Anna, told me over the years about her beloved father and the life and times of the family.

Contents

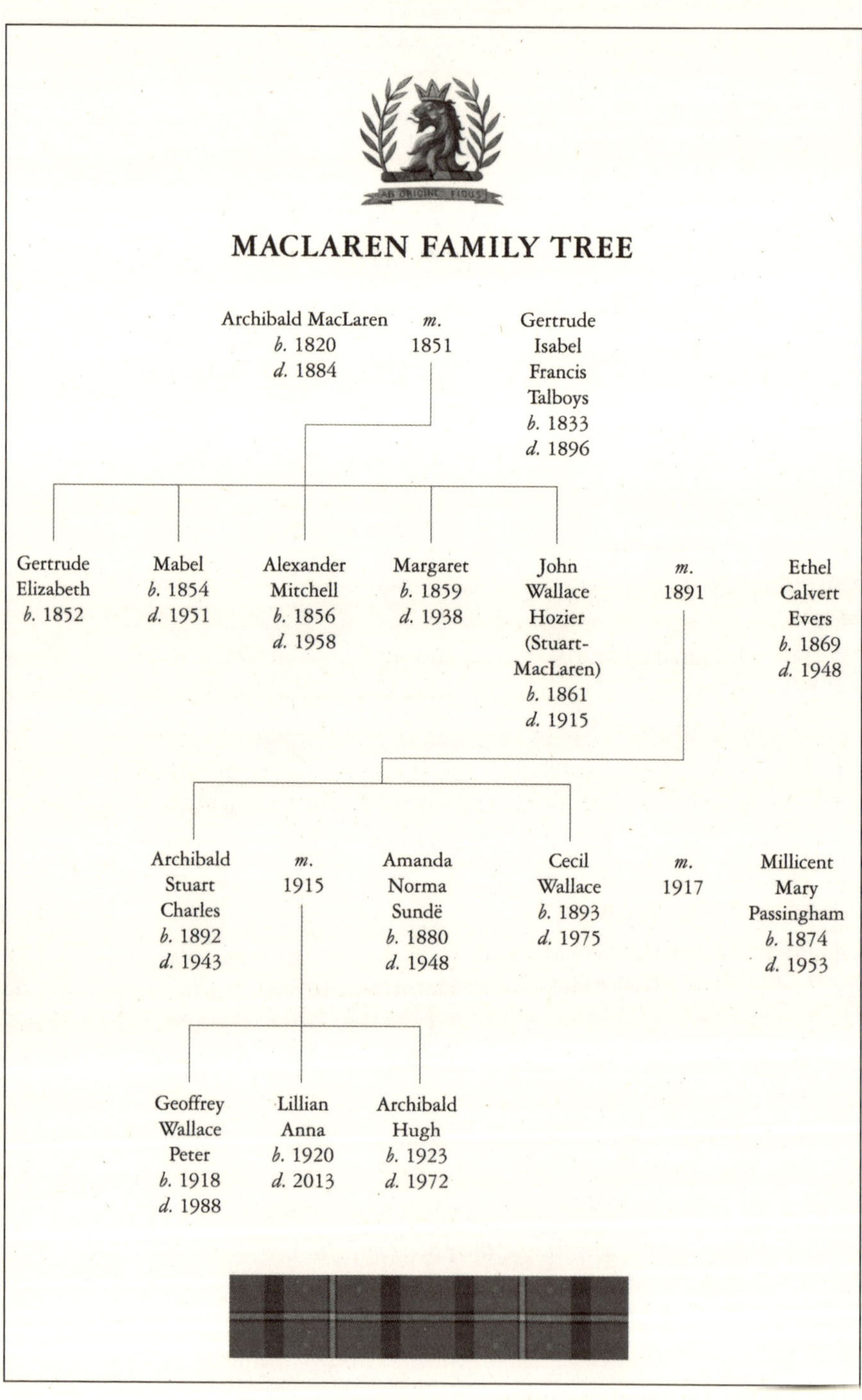

MacLaren family tree. (MacLaren family)

Introduction

Monday, 4 August 1924, at 0900, a Vickers Vulture amphibious biplane leaves west Kamchatka in Far Eastern Russia. Flying at 3,000 feet, the crew encounter huge fog banks, and as they near Bering Island, the fog becomes solid. Desperate to regain visibility, they rapidly descend to 100 feet only to find the fog dropped to the surface of a very rough sea. In the blinding rain, the pilot swerves suddenly, narrowly avoiding a cliff, and makes a last-ditch attempt to land. As he does so, both wingtips shatter, and the wings start to break up as he beaches the plane. The crew jump into the bitterly cold surf, struggling to hold the plane head on to the sea, as they contemplate the end of the British attempt to be the first men to fly round the world.

Eventually, a Russian wireless operator manages to make contact with the Royal Canadian Navy which sends out HMCS *Thiepval*, one of its battle-class naval trawlers. The ship takes the remains of the plane and the crew, three serving members of the RAF—Squadron Leader Archibald Stuart Charles Stuart-MacLaren (chief organiser and navigator), Flying Officer William Noble Plenderleith (pilot) and Sergeant William Herbert Andrews (flight engineer / fitter/rigger)—to safety on Vancouver Island.

It is now May 2019, and I—MacLaren's granddaughter—am in Sidney on Vancouver Island, making the emotional trip of a lifetime. The Vulture's propeller still hangs on the wall of the Officers Mess at the Canadian Forces Base, Esquimalt, in Victoria, and my aim is to try to get into the heart and mind of my grandfather, one of the greatest flying adventurers of his time.

Life today is very different to how things were in the early 1900s. Technology has transformed the way we live, and travelling round the world is far from the ordeal it once was. But it is only because of the pioneering spirits of so many people like my grandfather that the world has moved on to learn and achieve so much more.

I began to realise that I wanted to try to get back into the reality of my grandfather's soul, into his emotions and feelings—his adventurous spirit, his need to be a first achiever, his arrogance, his naughtiness and his everlasting ardent wish to make everything he achieved meaningful. As I sit and look out over the water to the snow-capped mountains beyond, I feel myself overwhelmed with feelings of empathy and longing—almost as though he is there inside my heart.

Archibald Stuart Charles Stuart-MacLaren was hardly ever mentioned by my parents when I was a child. Sadly, he died long before I had the chance to meet him. He was my grandfather on my maternal side and spoken of with great fondness by his daughter (my mother) Lillian Anna, when I finally asked her about his life. I discovered that a few of his precious mementoes stored in the attics of the many homes I had lived in during my childhood had gone with my elder brother, Simon John, to Australia, where he had emigrated many years before. Luckily for me, it was agreed that these family treasures should not stay in Australia, where probably no one would know anything about grandfather or his life and achievements. So, these pieces of memorabilia, including a silver replica of the Vulture aeroplane and the First World War medals gained from his distinguished career, were returned to England. This was quite a difficult task, as to lose these rare objects would have been calamitous, so many trips were made to bring them safely back—thus echoing the numerous journeys across the world which were to be a part of my grandfather's life.

It was then when I finally started to get to know a little bit more about someone who has now become a huge part of who I truly am. Over the years I have challenged my own thinking on so many aspects of life, and my research has drawn me into becoming an adventurer in my own right. I have crossed numerous continents to make discoveries, giving talks about grandfather's amazing ability to continually advance the knowledge of flying. I have also met fascinating people whose encouragement has led me into an all-encompassing wish to get his phenomenal life story out into the world.

This is where it all begins.

1

The MacLaren Family

The MacLaren family's imaginative sense of adventure was pivotal in shaping Archibald Stuart Charles's (Archie's) fascinating life—full of initiative and determination—as well as his enthusiastic and energetic character.

Archie's father, John Wallace Hozier MacLaren (1861–1915)—known as 'Tot' when he was a baby—was born into both a scholarly and physically adept family.[1] Archie's grandfather, Archibald MacLaren (1819–1894)—after whom Archie was named—was a teacher of physical education, gymnastics and fencing, which he studied in Europe, and later became the founder of the Oxford Gymnasium. He wrote several books on physical training, one of which was adopted by the British Army at a time when the empire was flourishing.[2] But he also had a 'gentler' side to him, and in 1857 he wrote a book of fairy stories (published in 1874) —a far cry from his military training manuals.[3] They were a collection of ballads and metrical tales illustrating the fairy mythology of Europe, and in writing them he stood up for the fairies and insisted that the little ones should not believe that their old friends had really been set aside by the scientific discoveries of those later days. These stories would have been very popular with the young people who were to be a great part of his life after he was married.

In 1864 Archibald and his second wife Gertrude Isobel Francis (née Talboys) (1833–1896) founded a preparatory school in Oxford called Summer Fields Preparatory School for Boys. Gertrude was a classical scholar and gifted teacher, and it was under her guidance that the school began to grow. The school motto, 'Mens sana in corpore sano', ('A healthy mind in a healthy body') very much reflected the characters of both Archibald and Gertrude.

Of their five children, John Wallace Hozier was their only son to survive childhood. In turn he would receive a first-class education. He started his school years at Summer Fields, and then at the age of 13, he gained a scholarship to Wellington College in Berkshire, where he was clearly a very successful scholar and sportsman, having learnt a great deal from his father. He played cricket, racquets, fives and rugby and was an active member of the natural science society and the debating society. He also wrote poems in Latin: one named 'Gladiatores'. [4]

John Wallace then went up to Magdalen College, Oxford in 1880, and after taking his BA he finally went on to Heidelberg and Berlin Universities, where he obtained a PhD. He then returned to Summer Fields and taught the increasing number of boys enrolled at the school. He also went on to be co-head for a second Summer Fields School—'Summers mi' at St Leonards-on-Sea, Sussex—for boys with delicate health who might benefit from the sea air. [5]

In 1891, John Wallace married Ethel Calvert Evers (1869–1948) who proved to be the guiding influence in their lives. They had two sons, Archibald Stuart Charles (my grandfather, Archie), born on 15 May 1892, and Cecil Wallace, born a year later. While both boys greatly loved their father, who was a cultured, gentle and scholarly man, they regarded their mother—a beautiful woman, tall and dominating—with much fear and trepidation. It seems that Ethel was never that keen on having children, much preferring to travel around the world, so she was a very strict and disciplined parent for such time that she and her husband spent with their children.

When Archie was born, Ethel's sister Mabel was to mark the occasion in a letter to their mother:

My dearest Mater,
Just a line to tell you Ethel had a little boy, or rather a huge big one, this afternoon at 5 o'clock and they are both very flourishing; we haven't seen Ethel yet, but the baby is not nearly as ugly as we expected, and I daresay will improve in a few days—I will write

you a postcard every day to let you know how she is. I <u>am</u> glad
it's all over, we have been up since 2 this morning and feel pretty
washed out. Poor old Wallace is trying to find a family likeness in
the baby's nails!

So, the fact that Archie grew to be very tall and handsome was clearly
noted at this early stage!

In 1903, the MacLaren's changed their surname by deed poll
to Stuart-MacLaren. This was possibly because Ethel thought it
fashionable to be double-barrelled. Alternately, it could have been
because John Wallace's father, Archibald, had married twice in his
native Scotland: after his first wife died, he married his late wife's
sister Gertrude, which under Scottish law at the time was not allowed.
By returning south of the border, John Wallace may have thought
that changing their surname wiped the slate clean, allowing them to
start afresh.[6]

Ethel was a great one for the social whirl and the family were
regular participants in the winter sports at what was then the Kurhaus
Seehof Hotel and Health Resort at Davos-Dorf in the Swiss Alps.
It was a place where many celebrities also came, including Charles
Wellington Furse, an English painter who 'in his short span of life
demonstrated such skill as a portrait and figure painter that he forms
an important link in the chain of British portraiture which extends
from the time when Van Dyck was called to the court of Charles 1
into the 20th century'.[7] Furse was to paint a portrait of Ethel which
still hangs in the dining hall at Summer Fields School.

Another interesting contact at the time in Davos could have been
Hugh Montague Trenchard, later to become the Father of the Royal
Air Force. A connection could well have been made by the family in
the early 1900s as Trenchard was convalescing in Switzerland after
being critically wounded in South Africa, and had been told that the
air was likely to be of benefit to his lungs. Boredom saw him take up
bobsleighing and he won the St Moritz Tobogganing Club's Freshman
and Novices' Cups in 1901, a remarkable triumph for someone who
had been unable to walk unaided only a few days before.[8]

Bobsleighing began in 1877 in Davos when people added a steering
wheel to a normal sled; the first bobsleighing club at St Moritz was

formed in 1897. Most of the first bobsleigh runs were snow-covered roads, and for years it was a popular recreational sport, particularly for the wealthy, very like skiing today. The sport's name comes from the way early teams 'bobbed' their heads to try to gain speed on straight portions of the run.

Tobogganing and bobsleighing were just coming into fashion in the early 1900s, and Ethel became the women's bobsleigh champion many years running. She was captain of her own team and bob sleigh—known as the 'Scarlet Runner'—and collected several gold and silver medals, as well as six broken ribs! *The Davos Courier, c.* 1930 records:

> We remember the MacLarens having in those days a home-made miniature ice-run at Dorf, on which their son Archie used to sharpen his sporting qualities, when he was not exercising on the Buol Run or on the 'historic' course to Klosters, where he afterwards achieved honours, following in his father's footsteps—or, rather, toboggan tracks. The MacLarens came pretty regularly to Davos until after the opening of the Schatzalp Run in 1907 (of which Mr MacLaren was one of the promoters), and Mrs MacLaren's famous 'Scarlet Runner' caused sensations on that course in the first few seasons.[9]

Ethel also took her husband on fantastic treks and safaris in the early 1900s—through the Middle East, India and Burma, and from Cairo to Cape Town—always taking their own car and chauffeur as well as Boris, her Great Dane. All this was recorded in the remarkable glass slides which were taken by John Wallace as he was dragged along beside her.

2

School Days

While all this bobsleighing and trekking round the world was going on, Archie and his brother Cecil were growing up. Naturally, they both went to Summer Fields School where they boarded, as they were not always included in their parents' travels.

With their parents constantly abroad on their world adventures, they were robbed of a proper and settled home life.

For such time as they did spend with their parents, it was known that both boys were very fond of their father, but were not close to their mother who was very strict with them. So, during the school holidays they did not enjoy much affection and unity of family life in their formative years.[1]

Archie's school career was to continue at Charterhouse School in Godalming, Surrey (Saunderites House), where he started in 1906, aged 14.[2] During his years there he was featured in many listings in the Charterhouse 'Black Book' which was taken around to every master on Wednesday mornings for them to make entries.[3]

Drill and copy lines were meted out fairly regularly to Archie for offences such as:

Date	Offence	Punishment
July 29 1908	Banco (*homework*) not done	Drill
Oct 14	No books, no banco	120 copy lines
Oct 17	Idle	Drill
Oct 24	Idle	Drill
Nov 11	Failing to come when told	Drill

Nov 18	No work, no book	Chapter to write out
Nov 28	Breaking rules	Drill
Dec 2	Persistently inattentive	Work set
Dec 5	Still very inattentive	Drill
Dec 16	Incessant chattering	150 copy lines
March 3 1909	Snowballing	Write copy lines
March 6	No banco done	Drill & 125 copy lines
March 17	Persistent unpunctuality	100 lines
April 6	Silly misbehaviour	Drill
May 26	Slippers at 12 o'clock	75 copy lines
June 16	Punishment not done	200 copy lines
July 3	Defiance	Drill
July 14	Disobedient	Work set
July 14	Disgracefully idle & impudent	100 copy lines
July 28	Misbehaviour	150 copy lines
July 31	Late for Chapel	Drill

One of the masters was to write to Archie's father on 25 December 1900. It is interesting that it was written on Christmas Day—Archie's parents were presumably once more in Davos and unlikely to have taken their sons, who were left behind to be looked after during the holidays by the masters back at Summer Fields School. The letter reads:

It is heart breaking to find Archie again miss promotion: one feels it is so easily within his reach, if only there were steadiness at the back of his abilities. I have done my best to stimulate him, but with poor result. The boy takes punishment with extraordinary humility, and amends for the time. Then some new priority wrecks him. All the little trifles (like slippers etc.) that ought to have been long outgrown, continually beset him. On the last Sunday, during Chapel at prayers he was blowing the boy's hair in front, often laughing for pleasure—nearly 16 is he not? And so it goes on. I do think there is improvement. Longer stretches of responsible behaviour and some realization of follies and considering what they have been, you may even derive encouragement from Reports: but the final place—19th—is altogether disappointing. He thought he had done 'nearly everything' right, in papers where he came badly to grief. I had hoped he might come up by seams, and make good the usual violent oscillations in weekly placings. He does take keen interest in his engineering work.[4]

As his life unfolds, this letter will bring back many of the characteristics which manifested themselves during these years.

While Archie's school life was in such a turmoil, his brother Cecil had quite a different attitude to learning. After Summer Fields, he won a King's Scholarship to Eton in 1907, and went on to New College, Oxford. Later, in the First World War, he joined the Royal Army Service Corps.

In 1908, Archie qualified in the Junior Division of the Officers Training Corps (OTC) at Charterhouse, and his total service was one year and two terms. His rank was private on resignation, and he had a qualification in musketry.[5]

The formation of the OTC was originally set up to investigate the problem of the supply of adequately trained officers for both the regular and reserve forces of the Army. It was proposed that it would have two divisions, the Junior Division being in schools. The hope was that it would attract young men into the Army and provide an efficient system of progressive military instruction for prospective officers.[6]

This qualification may have done Archie some good for his later career, although he was never actually awarded a certificate of proof at the time.

Archie was finally expelled from Charterhouse in cricket quarter 1909, aged 17, possibly for being caught smoking once too often and not attending roll call in the mornings, after having a night out in the town.[7]

Perhaps this early part of his life was to show him to be the adventurous, stubborn, highly intuitive and determined person that he demonstrated during the rest of his life. After all, he had been exposed thus far to an overabundance of discipline and tradition, while starved of love, affection and a settled home life.

It was also at this time that he met and fell in love with the beautiful young girl Violet Emily Dimble (aged 16). It was known that they wanted to marry but this was not to be allowed by Violet's parents, as she was considered too young. They were instructed to wait a couple of years, at which time they could reconsider, but this was not meant to be.

3

The Start of Adventures

As can be imagined, Ethel was extremely annoyed at her son's inability to be a good pupil at school. So, in 1911, 19-year-old Archibald Stuart Charles Stuart-MacLaren was sent off to attend the Agricultural Farm and Colonial School for gentlemen's sons at Bradley Court, Mitcheldean in Gloucestershire. He was listed there as an army student.[1]

This college was established in the early twentieth century and was used to prepare pupils for work in the colonies: home farming, land agency and estate management. As well as giving their pupils a general education, they were thrown into manual work and a great deal of outdoor life on their 140 acres of farmland.[2] Outdoor learning included dairy, poultry, fruit-growing and horticulture, and no doubt all this hard active work was seen as something which would keep Archibald busy and out of mischief.

With all this experience, Ethel then decided to send him away travelling, with £5 in his pocket, to 'make good'.[3] For the next two years, Archibald was to spend his time working on rubber plantations in the Malay States and South Java. The main source of capital for the rubber sector at that time came from Britain. Given the growing demand for car tyres, due to the huge rise in transport, there was plenty of hard work to be had. He also went on to be involved in fruit-growing in Canada, which he would talk of many years later when interviewed by a reporter in Winnipeg in 1924, after his attempted world flight.[4]

His daughter Anna was also to tell the story that one day he was sitting on the side of the road breaking up stones in Canada, when a beautiful Norwegian woman walked past—she was an enigma and was called the Merry Widow as she was very attractive and beautifully dressed. Her name was Amanda Norma Sunde. She saw Archibald and liked him, but he was not that interested because of his continuing love for Violet Dimble. But Norma had money then, and got him out of his difficulties.

In July 1914, at the start of the First World War, Archibald returned to England with Amanda by his side. The assassination of Archduke Franz Ferdinand of Austria had set off a chain of conflicts and Great Britain was a leading Allied power. The armed forces were greatly expanding and Archibald's drive to fight for king and country gave him the desire to become involved.

After their return to England, Archibald and Amanda were married on 20 January 1915 at the parish church of South Farnborough, Southampton. Archibald was then 22 years of age although Amanda obviously did not want her age known (she was several years older than him), as it is blacked out on their marriage certificate.

Just after they were married, there was great sadness for Archibald. His father, John Wallace, who was spending the winters in his villa at La Oratava in the Canary Isles, due to deteriorating health, died there on 16 February 1915, aged 53. His obituary spoke of:

> … his kindness of heart and a certain cheery optimism, combined with great personal charm of manner and a ready wit, causing him always to be a desired and much-sought-after companion. The present generation of boys (at Summer Fields School) have necessarily known less of him of late years, but … his death leaves a blank which will not readily be filled.[5]

Archibald had worshipped his father and there was no doubt that many of these exceptional traits had been handed down in his personality.

It did not take Archibald's mother long to re-marry: one year later she wed Cecil Alfred Armstrong, a friend of Wallace who had been instructed to look after Ethel when he died. As they had no great interest in Summer Fields, Ethel continued to lead a merry dance around the world with her new husband.

Now, with his usual vitality and energy, Archibald decided that he wanted to obtain a pilot's license.

The Royal Flying Corps (RFC) had been formed in England in 1912 by royal warrant as a corps of the army, and therefore had army ranks, regulations and procedures. The military had begun to see that there was potential to use aircraft as observation platforms, and as the First World War started, the RFC stepped in to undertake reconnaissance and artillery observation.

No one would be accepted into the Flying Corps unless he possessed a pilot's license: the certificate issued by the Federation Aeronautique International (FAI). The FAI certificate was known universally as the 'ticket' although cadets still had to undergo complete flying training.[6]

In order to obtain this pilot's licence, MacLaren attended the British Flying School at Le Crotoy in Northern France on the bay of the Somme. This school had been started by two French brothers, Rene and Gaston Caudron, who were living in northern Picardy and working on their father's farm in the Somme basin.

In 1908, they had watched the demonstration flights of the 'brave new world' of aviation and became so excited about the possibilities that they created a factory in the town of Rue in Northern France, close to their home and farm, where they built the first G.3 and G.4 aircraft for the French military.[7] They also established a civil and military flying school in February 1913 on the beaches of Le Crotoy to train specialists in every field of military aviation using planes such as the Sopwith Pup, Letord 2, Caudron R.4 and many others.

Fortunately, MacLaren's French was fairly fluent, and he passed all the tests and went on to train in a Caudron 5106 biplane. On 4 June 1915, he obtained his Royal Aero Club Certificate Number 1310 as an air mechanic 2nd class (from 1910, the Royal Aero Club, as the FAI's UK representative, issued aviator's certificates, which were internationally recognised).[8]

At that time, MacLaren also managed to obtain a 'Certificate of good moral character for the last 10 years' from Dr Charles Eccles Williams, D.D. (Oxon), Clerk in Holy Orders, who was a master at Summer Fields School. This would have helped to certify him as a fit and proper person for appointment to a commission in the branch of the special reserve of officers in the King's Own Scottish Borderers (KOSB) for which he would now apply. This was an infantry regiment of the British Army and part of the Scottish Division.

With his Scottish family background, MacLaren probably wanted to make this important connection, and in order to enter the RFC, pilots had to come from a branch of the army, as well as possess a flying certificate from the Royal Aero Club.

On 12 July 1915, MacLaren was commissioned into the 3rd Battalion of the KOSB as a second lieutenant (regular army, special reserve of officers) with immediate secondment to the RFC. This was a special reserve battalion, based in Edinburgh at the time, and largely involved in recruiting and training.[9] He would not have seen any active service at this time.

But there was no doubt that flying was the drive and stimulus in MacLaren's life, and on 14 August he proceeded to the airfield in the village of Upavon in Wiltshire, home of the Central Flying School (CFS), where he undertook advanced training in flying and technical subjects in order to become a pilot in the RFC. The aim of the CFS was to train professional war pilots for experimental and research flying, and MacLaren gained a great deal of experience in flying all 'BE'-model aircraft, small and large Martinsydes and Bristol Scout biplanes. Graduates could then carry out short cross-country flights at heights around 15,000ft, while the ground training included theory of flight, map reading, military and naval aviation history and aircraft repair.

After completing his formal pilot training at Upavon, MacLaren was duly confirmed on 25 September 1915 as a gazetted flying officer in the RFC, regimental number 2663. Now his and Amanda's lives would begin to change dramatically in the theatre of the First World War.

The Middle East Campaign

By late 1914, it was clear that the RFC would need to be enlarged from its current seven squadrons to compliment the massive expansion of the British Army to continue the combat of the war. Initially, their role was to undertake reconnaissance and artillery observation in order to support the army, but because of the shortage of aeroplanes and trained pilots at that time new squadrons were formed by bringing in small groups of semi-trained people around a nucleus of pilots from the RFC training squadrons.

One of the new squadrons formed in February 1915 at Shoreham, West Sussex was 14 Squadron which was used as a training school while preparing to be sent to France. However, it had become apparent that Turkey's entry into the war was threatening the critically important link with the empire by way of the Suez Canal, and that aerial reconnaissance could play a major role in assisting the army in the defence of the canal.[1] So, by autumn 1915, together with the crew of 17 Squadron and under the operational control of 5 Wing RFC, the pilots and planes of 14 Squadron were dispatched to Egypt.

…Second Lieutenant Archibald Stuart Charles Stuart-MacLaren, KOSB Special Reserve, and to be seconded, had by now been gazetted as a flying officer in the military wing of the RFC.[2] He was sent to 14 Squadron at Shoreham, immediately after qualifying, from where he accompanied the unit to the Middle East as a 'founder member'. No. 14 Squadron was nicknamed 'Winged Crusaders' and their motto, which appears on the badge, was 'I spread my wings and keep my promise'.

On 7 November, the personnel of HQ 5 Wing and 14 Squadron embarked on the Blue Funnel Liner RMS *Anchises* at Southampton and disembarked in Alexandria, Egypt twelve days later. MacLaren was on board, accompanied by his wife Amanda and their Maltese terrier Tiny.

The equipment and aeroplanes, which included BE2c biplanes, arrived in crates on the SS *Hunsgrove* a few days later and were taken in their crates by rail to Heliopolis, just outside Cairo, where they were reassembled. The flights were based in different areas—'A' flight at Ismailia, which was the headquarters aerodrome. This was a small French town on the bank of Lake Timsah on the Nile Delta which was known as 'the city of beauty and enchantment'.[3] 'B' Flight was based at Heliopolis outside Cairo and 'C' Flight at Kantara on the Suez Canal. They were under the command of Lieutenant Colonel Geoffrey Salmond who had trained at the CFS at Upavon, where MacLaren had qualified.

The men followed a week later, and when they arrived in Heliopolis, everyone was allowed some time to get used to the warmer winter weather of Egypt, as well as to gain an understanding of where all the flights were based. Lines of white tents for the officers and men bordered the airfield. Amanda clearly thought she would be playing golf, perhaps with other officer's wives.

Amanda would most likely have been staying in one of the large hotels in Cairo, possibly Shepheard's Hotel. Archibald probably had more knowledge than most of this part of the world, as his parents would have told him many stories of their own travels there in years gone by.

No. 14 Squadron was now engaged in patrolling the Sinai desert to provide forewarning of any Turkish attacks as well as taking photographs which would provide the basis for the maps used by the army during its advances. Additionally, air attacks were carried out against Turkish troops and installations in the Sinai, and to start with MacLaren would probably have been flying French seaplanes, which he would have been accustomed to from his original training at the British Flying School in Northern France.

Shortly after Christmas 1915, 14 Squadron was relieved in Heliopolis by 17 Squadron and moved on to their headquarters aerodrome in Ismailia. This was a much easier place to be, as the harsh environment of the desert was now replaced by shade and tropical luxuriousness.

In February 1916, 14 Squadron had several BE2c biplanes, with a few Bristol Scouts to act as escorts, and were operating from Ismailia as well as from Heliopolis and Kantara. The BE2c was used primarily for reconnaissance work and photography, but its lack of manoeuvrability and restricted field of fire from the observer's front cockpit earned it the nickname 'Fokker Fodder', given its vulnerability to the German Fokker Eindecker monoplanes, in regular use at that time.[4] They were now settling into the routine of the defence of the Suez Canal, and 'C' Flight at Kantara, where MacLaren was now based, was commanded by Captain Harold Blackburn who had also trained at the CFS.

However, it seems that the relentless climate conditions in Egypt had caused MacLaren some problems from the start. The information and casualty forms issued by the army at the time recorded that he had been granted sick leave in January 1916 and was admitted to hospital in Cairo with slight jaundice and discharged a few weeks later.[5] This happened several times over the following months, and he was admitted to hospital again in Port Said, at the northern end of the Suez Canal, as well as Ismailia. Health problems would continue to beset him at many times in his career, and no doubt flying open cockpit planes in difficult weather conditions over the years took its toll.

Despite these occasional difficulties, in the early hours of 24 April, MacLaren, together with seven other aircraft from 'A' and 'C' Flights, flew a forty-minute flight to Qatiya to attack the Turks and drive them out of Sinai. The enemy was very thick on the ground, numbering about 1,000 with camels and horses; the men were in large groups and formed easy targets. Fifty-six 20lb bombs were dropped, Lewis guns were used to strafe the troops and the camp was completely destroyed.[6]

Afterwards, Captain Blackburn wrote a report from Kantara naming 2nd Lieutenant MacLaren as one of the officers engaged in the raid, and noting:

I wish to commend these officers… for the cool and highly efficient manner in which they have carried out the duties given them, showing initiative in addition to carrying out implicitly their instructions for the three bomb raids they have carried out in these two days.[7]

Lieutenant Colonel Salmond also recognised MacLaren's bravery, and in a letter home to his wife wrote:

His was a wonderful feat. We have photography of the burnt machine on the ground![8]

By mid-1916, 14 Squadron was fully operating in support of the army advance across Sinai. Frequent attacks were mounted against Turkish military installations, including the interception of Turkish water supplies and attacks against aerodromes, and MacLaren was once more involved in many of these raids.

Each flight had a daily written report of what had happened during the flying time, and MacLaren, flying in a BE2c No. 2118 and acting as observer on this occasion, reported:

No fresh tracks seen—5 or 6 Arabs, 2 flocks of goats and 10-15 camels grazing about one mile to the South East—the trenches are almost completely filled in—several men were working in one of the trenches, who looked as if they might be excavating—dropped message to O.C. Troops.[9]

While MacLaren was flying in Egypt, he was working with an observer, Major H. Cunningham Morris of the Royal Canadian Air Force, who had been transferred to Egypt in command of a naval aircraft section associated with the Royal Flying Corps. Years later, Cunningham Morris wrote some reports for the Calgary Daily Herald in Canada, as he wished to show the human side of MacLaren's career:

From a psychological point of view, MacLaren stood out as different from all others, and while being a thoroughly efficient and trained pilot, he seemed to have a soul above the ordinary work of handling his joystick, controlling his engine and the multiplicity of technical duties of a modern aviator; in other words, flying to him was something more than being master of a comprehensive mass of wood and steel.

During the Egyptian campaign of the Great War, when the day's work was done and the camp had retired, to the seclusion of its tents, MacLaren would, in moments of confidence, discuss deeper subjects, and dilate on the psychology of flying and the more advanced sentiments that lay behind the conquest of the air. How vividly one can call to mind those quiet conversations under the purple Egyptian nights, and MacLaren's almost inspired description of his feelings when in control of a big aeroplane.

There is, he said to me on one occasion, something majestic and stable about the big bombers which a pilot learns to love, either in heavy work, joy riding the heavens or sight-seeing among the clouds. An exquisite community grows up between machine and pilot; each, as it were, emerges into the other. The machine is rudimentary and the pilot the intellectual force. The levers and the controls are the nervous system of the machine, through which the will of the pilot may be expressed—and expressed to an infinitely fine degree. A flying-machine is something entirely apart from and above all other contrivances of man's ingenuity.

The aeroplane is the nearest thing to animate life that man has created. In the air, a machine ceases, indeed, to be a mere piece of mechanism; it becomes animate and becomes capable not only of primary guidance and control, but actually of expressing a pilot's temperament.

The lungs of a machine, its engines, are again the crux of man's wisdom. Their marvellous reliability and great intricacy are almost as awesome as the human anatomy. When the engines are going well and synchronized to the same speed, the roar of the exhausts develops into one long-sustained rhythmical boom-boom-boom. It is a song of pleasant harmony to the pilot, a symphony of contentment and sings of perfect firing and says that 'all is well'.

But on the other side of the picture is the extraordinary courage and determination of the man in the carrying out of his duties. He never entered upon a task blindly or half-cognizant of the details of the task allotted him. His plan of action was always ready and the way paved for a safe return, as far as human skill and endurance would allow. Combined with that dash and vim was a tender-hearted sympathetic nature which won for him many friends, while a 'swelled head' was never his, but an almost pathetic anxiety to disappear from the limelight.

During the leisure hours after mess, before retiring for the nights to their tents many arguments were developed by the R.F.C. squadron embracing various subjects. During one of these discussions MacLaren gave it as his opinion that it might be a good idea to practise bomb dropping without actually using, and therefore wasting unnecessarily ammunition. He made a suggestion to his commanding officer that on the next bombing practice, oranges instead of bombs should be employed.

Accordingly, the following morning, armed with several large bags full of this delectable fruit, MacLaren spent an hour or two in the air dropping the oranges from different heights on to the target placed in the sand, and noting the effect on the sighting. Interested on-lookers standing near the target declared that in some instances the impact of the oranges was so great as to break stout pieces of timber and even bend metal rods.

So pleased was MacLaren over the success of his new innovation, that whenever bombing practice was the order of the day, he used to load up the machine with his fruit, little dreaming how important a part in the war they were soon to play.

About this time the Turks were becoming more aggressive and arrogantly on the offensive, and it was learned from our intelligence service that a big attack on the Suez Canal was being planned. Consequently, aerial reconnaissances were carried out daily which showed that the enemy were strengthening their position and extending their trenches.

MacLaren in describing his experiences said: "After circling over my objective, a particularly well entrenched position, with several strong points where the Turks had recently extended their lines, I decided that my principal attack should be launched at this section and from there down the successive series of communicating trenches, where, even if my bombs did not make direct hits, they would nevertheless do considerable damage and prevent the enemy from concentrating their '"push"' from this point.

"I then commenced to drop my 'eggs' three or four bursting almost directly over the 'strong point', and as far as I could see, with terrible and effective results. The Turkish gunners soon got my range, and I had an uncomfortable few minutes until I could climb to a higher altitude, clear of the anti-aircraft fire and resume my attack.

"Then to my consternation I found that my bomb release had jammed and that as far as being any more an effective fighting machine, I was out of the running. I knew that the Turkish morale had had a severe shaking that morning and during the last few days, and that it would not take much to create a panic in the trenches and, remembering that I had several bags of oranges in my plane left over from my last practice, I decided on a wild plan to swoop down to about a thousand feet and drop them, as I had done on my practice targets, on to the fast-weakening Turks, hoping that perhaps the effect of something falling from an aeroplane, and bursting, might bring about the final coup.

"The scheme exceeded my wildest hopes, for after a hail of fruit over the enemy's lines, and much of it must have taken some effect or other, judging by the commotion that followed, I saw the Turks swarming out of their trenches and scampering in a stampede over the sand back to their reserve lines.

I could hardly believe my eyes when I saw the Turks streaming from their dugouts, covering their faces with their hands as my oranges scattered their contents far and wide, striking with tremendous force and I am convinced that but few of the Turkish soldiers realized just what hit them."

It is not given to every airman to be so resourceful or to fight his battles with fruit for his ammunition, but MacLaren was quick to realise that speedy action, in the demoralised condition the Turks were in, was necessary and so took a chance, which was crowned with incredible success.[10]

Despite the passage of time, MacLaren never forgot his mother. He was able to write home to her from time to time, knowing she would have been pleased to have his view of how things were in Egypt and to be able to compare how different it was to how it had been in the early 1900s when she was there on her Grand Tour. One letter he wrote on 4 May 1916 shows a very down-to-earth picture of how his life could have been ended at any one moment:

May 4th/1916   No 14 Squadron
                                                          R.F.C.
                                                          B.M.E.F.

My dearest Mother,

Thank you so much for your nice letter of the 14th April, which I have just received. I am so sorry that I haven't written to you for such a long time. We have been most awfully busy of late. However that is no excuse. I hope you got my last letter alright enclosing the snapshots. Some of them were quite decent. I shall probably be able to send you some more next week.

I am afraid you don't like Switzerland very much now. It must be horrid with nearly everyone more or less pro-German. Why don't you go home to England for the summer. It will be nice and warm for you there.

I am enclosing a cutting out of the Egyptian mail. I took part in all those bombing raids and also took part in the battle of Katia: you nearly lost your son in that battle. I came down to 800 feet and opened fire on the Turks with a machine-gun, and in return got thirty bullets through my aeroplane, one of which went clean through my seat and tore my coat right up the back and another grazed my leg. However it was real good fun. Flying is even better fun than bobbing. Perhaps one of these days I may be able to take you up for a flight. I wish we could get a little snow out here for a change. I am simply cooking and the flies are awful....

Well mother dear, there is very little news to give you. I will try and write you a longer letter next week. Give my love to everyone.

                                         Lots of love, ever yr loving
                                                          Archie

MacLaren's mention of his 'near death experience' to his mother, was also written about by Cunningham-Morris:

On many occasions the writer learned from MacLaren how great was the inspiration of the presence of his wife in Egypt, which became one of his strongest moral helps and how in every "stunt" the element of risk and danger disappeared under the spell of her influence. Her carefully protected portrait occupied a prominent place among the many and varied "gadgets" with which his machine was equipped, and on one occasion was instrumental in practically saving his life.

Saved by photo frame

On Easter Sunday, and incidentally St Georges Day, during the Egyptian campaign a handful of British troops totalling about 800, encamped toward the Turkish Front at Katia on the Sinai Peninsula, were attacked in the early dawn by an army of over 3,000 Turks undercover of a fog. At the first onslaught 400 of our men were cut down, while the remaining 400 launched a counter attack against the enemy so suddenly and vigorously that they succeeded in completely disorganising the Turks, and the unprecedented scene of less than 400 British soldiers charging an army—just such another famous deed as "the charge of the Light Brigade" in Crimean days— was enacted on the Libyan desert. The Turks fled in panic-stricken disorder like a great host over the desert, before the great rush of this handful of khaki-clad soldiers, while bombs and machine guns from our aeroplanes, arriving in the nick of time completed the work of demoralisation, and the British airmen led by MacLaren, swooped down almost onto the sand and skimming low raked the fleeing Turks with a deadly hail of bullets.

The writer, engaged in another sector of the fight, did not get much opportunity of seeing MacLaren until after the affair was over, but it was learned that a shot from a Turkish rifle had hit his machine, entering through the fuselage, and the direction clearly in line with the pilot's head. The bullet, in its death-dealing mission struck the metal edge of the framed portrait, damaging the picture, but being so deflected that it missed MacLaren's head by only an inch or two.[11]

Then, on 13 June, a retaliatory raid was ordered on El Arish Aerodrome, in the north-eastern sector of the Sinai Peninsula, with

MacLaren and two other aircraft tasked with entrapping an elusive German aeroplane out of the hanger in order to destroy it, as well as photographing the exact location of the aerodrome. A report was issued after the attack:

> Whilst engaged in the bombardment of El Arish Aerodrome on the 13th instant, 2/Lieut A. S. MacLaren, No 14 Sqdn, accompanied by 2/Lieut H.H. James, No 14 Sqdn, as Observer, saw a Fokker machine climbing up towards them. This machine was quite new and climbed with great rapidity. When it reached to within 500 feet below our machine, it opened fire, firing through the propeller and hitting our machine.
>
> The pilot at once realised that the machine was one of the Fokker ones, and swerved so as to keep above and behind the hostile machine, thus preventing him aiming at his machine. Although the German gained height and again turned in order to get his propeller facing towards our machine, 2/Lieut. MacLaren out-manoeuvred him every time, whilst at the same time 2/Lieut. James poured a steady machine gun fire into the German machine. This fight occurred at 7,000 feet. The Fokker dived steeply, pursued by our machine, which it escaped owing to its greater diving speed. At one time during the engagement, the machines were not more than 50-70 feet apart.[12]

Lieutenant Colonel Salmond reported that the attack on El Arish, with the help of the Navy, was wonderful:

> It was undoubtedly the first aerial attack from the sea that has ever been made. I was lucky to have the sea to help me....everyone is very pleased out here...and MacLaren who blew up the German machine, has been given a Military Cross. His was a wonderful feat.[13]

There was no doubt that MacLaren was never afraid to just charge into the fray at any given time, and his daring and sense of adventure (which he no doubt inherited from his mother) was critical in his ability to be 'truly brave'.[14]

The *London Gazette* 29684 of 27 July 1916 read:

> His Majesty the King has been graciously pleased to confer the Military Cross on the under-mentioned officers and warrant officers, in recognition of their gallantry and devotion to duty in the field:

> 2nd Lieutenant A. S. C. MACLAREN, K.O. Scot. Bord. Special Reserve, and R.F.C. For conspicuous gallantry. On approaching an aerodrome he observed a hostile aeroplane on the ground preparing to start, with pilot and observer in their seats and mechanics holding onto the wings. He descended to 100ft., dropped a bomb squarely into the machine and blew it up, together with the pilot, observer and mechanics. He then attacked and set fire to a Fokker, which was in a hanger.

Now there was no stopping MacLaren's need for intrepid achievement.

The RFC mounted a major raid on El Arish aerodrome on 18 June, and the route from Kantara, as before, involved flying over the sea with navy trawlers on station to provide rescue cover should it be needed. There were eleven aircraft engaged in this raid, one of which was a single-seater flown by MacLaren of 'C' Flight. The aircraft took off at 0623 followed the coast about a mile out to sea and climbed to 7,000 ft with the intention of attacking El Arish from the south-east. The first aircraft over the target was MacLaren at 0800.

As he dived towards the hangers, he noticed that a Rumpler biplane was starting up just outside its hangar. In order not to miss his target, he flew down to 100 ft and released three bombs. One hit the enemy aircraft fair and square, blowing it to pieces and killing the aircraft crew as well as wounding the ground crew in attendance. MacLaren then went on to drop more bombs on several more of the hangers.

On the afternoon of 2 August, MacLaren and his observer of the day 2nd Lieutenant T. J. West, set off from Port Said in a de Havilland Airco DH.1A '4609', a two-seater biplane with a 'pusher' propeller mounted at the rear, to escort a BE2c carrying out a reconnaissance mission. West sat in the front of the open cockpit to maximise the field of fire while MacLaren sat behind and controlled the aeroplane. These biplanes only saw operational service in the Middle East theatre of war and were primarily used as escorts for the BE2 reconnaissance aircraft.

However, on this occasion MacLaren once again showed his fortitude and courage, scoring the first Allied victory on the Egyptian front when he and West sent a German Aviatik two-seater biplane down near to Bir Salmana. The enemy crew, Lieutenant H. Henkel and Obit Stalter, were taken prisoner.

Cunningham-Morris once again wrote about MacLaren's many expeditions:

On many occasions I accompanied MacLaren on his many expeditions against the Turks, acting as observer, and never once did he falter or waiver when prompt action was required to carry out the work assigned to him or risk his machine or its living freight. MacLaren soon became a marked man by the Otterman forces, who would dearly loved to have captured this youthful thorn in their flesh, but each adventure against the Turkish lines saw the safe return of the intrepid airman to whom duty was second nature and modesty a virtue.

On one memorable morning in the summer of 1916, I took my seat in the observers compartment of the de Havilland bombing aeroplane piloted by MacLaren, our objective being the Turkish stronghold of El Arish, near the Palestine border, the last fortified city in the hands of the enemy, in their steady retreat from the Sinai Peninsula, driven back by the relentless advance of British arms.

Dawn had scarcely opened over the eastern rim of the desert when our machine left the aerodrome at El-Kantara (Suez Canal), and MacLaren, knowing that time was precious, as well as the mysterious half light which he hoped would be a screen against the sharp eyes of the Turkish patrols, and that El Arish was far away, began to climb steeply so as to reach a height of four or five thousand feet before setting his course for the Turkish stronghold, a hundred or so miles away, to the north east.

The camp of the British divisions was soon lost to sight in the violent haze that hung over the limitless desert, pre-engaging the approach of dawn, and with the engines purring their 2000 revolutions in faultless precision, the miles melted away behind us. As the red ball of the sun burst into a flaming glory over the low desert hills, the domes and minarets of El Arish appeared through the fast thinning mist, catching the sun's first rays in a hundred points of fire.

In a few minutes we were over the city, which lay spread out beneath us in a congested mass, and as we circled round ever descending in order to ascertain the position of vital places for attack, sudden deafening explosions, unpleasantly near us, warned us that the Turks had spotted us and had made a pretty correct guess of our range.

With our eyes glued to our field glasses (so perfectly adjusted was the machine that the pilot could let go of the joy stick for short periods), we managed to locate what we thought were barracks, arsenals, fortified posts and other vital places.

Banking deeply, MacLaren circled up again to 5000ft, while I busied myself with adjustment of the bomb dropping sights, and at his signal I loosed off one of our six 60lb bombs, quickly followed by the others as we circled the city. Even at that height the roar of the explosions made our eardrums crack, and that our shots had proved effective was soon shown by heavy clouds of smoke that poured from several points in the vicinity of the areas we had located.

We were now being constantly shot at by the Turkish gunners, and to stay where we were any longer was asking for trouble, and our bombs having been dropped, there was nothing left but to return home. But MacLaren, fired by the excitement of the battle and the obvious success of our attack, passed a note to me to the effect that he intended to descend to a lower altitude, and ascertain if possible the extent of the damage done by our bombs.

Never shall I forget that descent, an almost perpendicular nose dive and spiral at tremendous speed, right over the city from which guns were still belching forth shrapnel and shells busting thickly around us. Like a bird our plane sped through the hall of death, an occasional ripping crashing sound telling us of torn canvas and splitting wood. Down, down we flew and it was a miracle that the vital parts of our machine were never hit. This city rose up to meet us, the streets alive with panic stricken people running here and there, while volumes of smoke and flame from several parts, and masses of ruined buildings showed that our bombs had done their work.

Almost before the Turks had time to realise that the enemy plane was actually in their midst and adjust their gun sights, MacLaren had begun to climb again vertically, the clamour and shouting of the astonished populace, the roar of flames and the crackle of rifle fire growing fainter and fainter as we rose and circled up to safety from the guns below.

But our work was done although it needed some hours to noon, and I turned to see what MacLaren was going to do. The joy stick was now unattended, the plane now headed for home, flying as though guided by some unseen hand. Both MacLaren's hands held a battered and fearsome looking object, but which nevertheless seemed to create a look of rapture on the young pilot's face as he gazed at it—the woolly mascot, the gift of his young wife, a symbol of luck, which he always carried on his flights. As MacLaren lifted his face, his eye caught mine and with a smile of utter contentment, pride and relief, and with a far-away look on his countenance, his lips were pressed to the impossible face of the woolly guardian, while the engines in perfect unison sang a paean of victory.[15]

But at this time, the military authorities of the British expeditionary force were not keen upon the presence of women in the war zone and a mandate came forth, gently yet firmly, insisting that they leave Egypt. This command was obeyed, but the news came as a hard blow to MacLaren who was happy in the presence of his wife near the scene of his activities, yet safe in Port Said, which was practically immune from Turkish attack. But so great was his faith in the inspiration of his wife, that the authorities, perhaps for the first time on record in the history of a British army in the field, allowed sentiment to take the place of cold officialdom and permitted Amanda to stay in Egypt. But she must leave Port Said for the safer haven of Cairo.

Cunningham Morris escorted her down to Cairo, where she was well out of the danger zone yet within reach of the man who worshipped the very ground she walked on, and where her very presence, perhaps unknown to herself, would be instrumental in inspiring 'her man' to deeds of valour and devotion to duty.

She was clearly imbued with the same sense of courageousness as her husband, as on one occasion, while still in Port Said before moving to Cairo, a number of women and children were injured during a bombing by a hostile aeroplane. Amanda, regardless of her own safety, was one of the first to enter the street, even when bombs were still being dropped, and render what first aid she could to the poor injured Arab children, securing their removal to hospital and safety.

MacLaren was now awarded a bar to his Military Cross for subsequent acts of conspicuous gallantry:

2nd Lt. A. S. C. MacLaren, M.C., K.O. Sco. Bord.
He attacked and brought down an enemy machine from a height of 5,000 ft. He has on many previous occasions done very fine work.[16]

MacLaren was also mentioned in dispatches with a list of RFC officers whose work was extremely arduous and exhausting during the whole period: many pilots and observers were out two or three times a day for several consecutive days under very accurate anti-aircraft fire and were frequently engaged in air combats with enemy machines of superior power.[17]

Life was now to change for MacLaren as the RFC was being reorganised and 14 Squadron's direct offensive action in Sinai came to an end. On 17 September 1916 he was posted to 23 Squadron in Aboukir, near Alexandria, with Amanda and Tiny accompanying him. This was a reserve squadron equipped with BE2c and BE2e aeroplanes which was set up as a unit for advanced training. With all his previous courage, daring and experience, MacLaren would have been the perfect pilot to be able to train others in what they might expect when out on a mission.

By February 1917, he was then signed off as captain for 23 Squadron on a pilot's transfer card, meaning he would now have been a flight commander. With his usual fluidity of life, and probably another wish for adventure, that March he was to send a letter from the headquarters of the 20th Reserve Wing of the RFC in Aboukir to the Director of Air Organisation, Air Board Office in the Strand, London with an unusual request:

CONFIDENTIAL   ABOUKIR 13-3-17
Headquarters,
20th. Reserve Wing,
Royal Flying Corps.

Sir,
Having heard that there will be a certain number of vacancies for appointment in the Japanese Army after the war of Officers of the British Army as Instructors of Aviation, I have the honour to submit this, my application, for the consideration of such an appointment. I have spent approximately 3½ years out East, and to a certain extent, understand the customs of the East.

> I have the honour to be, Sir, Your obedient Servant.
> A Stuart-MacLaren, M.C. Capt. R.F.C.

The Anglo-Japanese Alliance bound Britain and Japan to assist one another in safeguarding their respective interests in China and Korea and was directed against Russian expansionism in the Far East. MacLaren's request was considered in case an occasion would arise to employ him.

However, nothing came of it, and on 18 April 1917, Archibald, Amanda and Tiny embarked on a British steamer to return to England. He was now 25 years old, and on arrival back in Croydon it was clear that he still had some medical problems. On examination by the air medical board in Croydon on 17 July, it was found that:

He is subject to attacks of malaria, which he originally developed in Malay states in 1913. Has done most of his flying in Egypt where he had no difficulty in flying. Since returning to England he finds that flying at any altitude above 7,000 feet brings on an attack of malaria; he considers this due to cold. Last attack 6 weeks ago, lasting 3-4 hrs only. 6 days ago had attack of ptomaine poisoning with vomiting and colicky pains. These are now better. Has some superficial sores on buttocks which are nearly healed. His general condition is good.[18]

MacLaren was, of course, very eager to get back to flying once again, so after a month's rest staying at the Strand Palace Hotel in London, the board found that he had recovered and was able to fly without any discomfort.

There was no doubt that new adventures were on the horizon.

The Start of the Royal Air Force and Flight to Egypt

Fortunately for MacLaren, his full flying pay was now returned to him (after his time off due to illness), and Major E. G. R. Lithgow R.A.M.C., president of the medical board, notified the Air Ministry that he was fit for flying, although not above 5,000ft, as his disabilities had been caused by the effect of high flying.

So, in August 1917 notice came from the medical board with the request: 'Please board Captain MacLaren as a special case. This officer is required for service in Egypt.' He was once again to embark on a troopship which left Marseilles, France on 11 September, arriving at Port Said, Egypt ten days later.

Very little is known about his time here, as there are many gaps in the service records, but there is no doubt that MacLaren had been recalled to Egypt for having shown such courage, initiative and intuitive sense in his previous years with 14 Squadron. Now he would be needed to instruct new pilots, as there was still an urgent need to train local cadets, along with those coming in from South Africa.[1]

No. 3 School of Military Aeronautics was providing theoretical instruction to prospective aircrew and had opened at Aboukir, a town on the coast of Egypt, in November 1916. It then moved to Abbassia, Cairo in February 1917 before settling at the Palace Hotel, Heliopolis that October.[2] Captain MacLaren began training pilots on 30 September. He was placed at 196 Training Unit, which had been formed in Heliopolis in August but was disbanded three months later to become part of The Aerial Fighting School.[3]

Now a flight commander, he was then transferred to 22 Reserve Squadron/Training Squadron (RS/TS) at Aboukir, where intermediate training was being given on Avro 504 biplanes and Curtiss JN-3 training planes. Finally, he was moved on to 23 RS/TS, where he gave advanced training on BE2c and BE2e biplanes. He had already trained on these planes at The British Flying School at Le Crotoy in 1915, as well as flying them in his courageous efforts to suppress the enemy bombardments in Egypt during the previous months.

While all this was going on, the MacLaren family was growing. Archibald and Amanda's first son, Geoffrey Wallace Peter (known as Wallace), was born in Hyeres, Toulon, South East France on 31 January 1918. An extract from the French register of civil status states that his father, of English origin, was a Captain of the English Army, while his mother, without profession, was domiciled at the Grand Hotel des Iles d'Or in the town of Hyeres.

Why Amanda was in France for the birth is completely unknown. Perhaps she had stopped off there when she and Archibald had returned from Egypt—after all, the records showed that Archibald boarded the troopship back to Egypt from Marseilles the previous September, so maybe they had friends or family members there to support her. Amanda and her baby then returned to London after the birth.

However, ill health was still to have an impact on MacLaren and there is no doubt that at the time—with the desert heat, the engine noise of open-cockpit planes and ongoing bouts of malaria contracted in the Malay States—he was feeling the effects.

On 24 March 1918 a letter from the deputy adjutant general of the Egyptian Expeditionary Force arrived at the War Office in London to announce that 2nd Lieutenant (T/Capt) MacLaren had sailed back to the UK on 16 February on the troopship HT *Abbasich*.[4] Now he would be able to meet his newborn son!

It was around this time—on 1 April 1918—that the Royal Air Force (RAF) was formed by amalgamating the RFC, run by the British army, and the Royal Naval Air Service (RNAS), operated by the Royal Navy. The aim was to make the use of airpower more efficient by ending the competition for new aircraft, pilots and support staff.

This new military service would be regulated by the newly formed government-controlled Air Ministry under Secretary of State for Air Winston Churchill. All officers attached to either the RFC or RNAS were therefore transferred to the RAF.[5]

Its Latin motto 'Per Ardua Ad Astra' has two meanings: 'through struggle to the stars' or 'through adversity to the stars', which was preferred by the RAF.

Second Lieutenant Archibald Stuart Charles Stuart-MacLaren, MC KOSB joined the RAF on 1 April 1918 as captain and was given the official service number 2663. The pay scale was roughly £250 a year for a lieutenant, with an additional list of separation allowances for wives and children. He was then promoted to major on 9 April.

The fact that the RAF started on April Fools' Day—and that MacLaren had a No.13 at the top of his certificate (not always the easiest of numbers)—could perhaps have had implications on his future career! At that time, it was also considered unlucky to sit thirteen people at one table, and many pilots were not happy with flying planes with numbers that added up to thirteen.

So far in his career, MacLaren had been flying fairly small aircraft, and bombing was only achieved in Egypt by using hand grenades or light bombs, as there would have been difficulty taking off if anything heavier was carried. Given this experience, in May 1918 he was posted to command 122 Squadron, which had been formed at Sedgeford Aerodrome in Great Yarmouth as a training squadron. The plan was to mobilise a day-bomber unit for deployment to France in September 1918, but it never became operational and was disbanded on 17 August.

MacLaren then came into contact with Brigadier General Amyas Eden Borton DSO (or 'Biffy' as he was known). Biffy had been in charge of the entire RFC Palestine Brigade in 1917 and had come back to England on leave in May 1918 intending to return to his base in Palestine by air. He had proposed to the Air Council that flying aircraft from England, rather than shipping them out in crates, would give a great advantage of speed. He also wanted to be able to show the commercial possibilities of civil aviation.

The RAF were concerned with the problem of maintaining its bases in Egypt and India when the war ended and thought that a ferry service of machines and men, together with spares, could be set up between England and Cairo. It felt that the route for such a service should be explored in collaboration with the Allied governments of France and Italy, although the purpose of the flight was not at that time to be disclosed.[6]

However, the Air Ministry took some time reaching a decision and did not accept Borton's proposal until 3 July, which gave him little time to arrange the flight before having to return to Palestine. The aircraft that was chosen for this flight was a Handley Page 0/400 twin-engine heavy bomber biplane aircraft. At that time, it was the largest aircraft ever produced in the United Kingdom and had already seen considerable service at the front.

While awaiting the Air Ministry's decision, Borton went over to France to visit the Handley Page squadrons in action there. Once his plan was finally accepted by Chief of the Air Staff Major General Sir Frederick Sykes, Borton was sent to RAF Cranwell in Lincolnshire where he met up with MacLaren, who—unlike Biffy—was already a Handley Page pilot, having been trained by Canadian Flight Lieutenant Harry Yates to handle the giant bomber. MacLaren was therefore the perfect person to accompany Borton on this pioneering flight.

A previous pioneering long-distance flight in a Handley Page 0/100 plane in May 1917 had been achieved from Manston airfield, Kent to Mudros Island in the Aegean Sea via France, Italy and Greece to Constantinople by Squadron Commander Kenneth Savory DSO. This had set the world record of nearly 2,000 miles for a cross-country flight to date. Both Borton and MacLaren spent time researching the report, diaries and maps that Savory had prepared, and they also met up with him and his co-pilot, Flight Lieutenant MacLelland, from whom they obtained a considerable amount of first-hand information which would be of great assistance.

The plane for the journey to Egypt was Handley Page 0/400 No. C9681, and Borton and MacLaren were to be accompanied by Flight Sergeant Raymond George Goldfinch (fitter) and Air Mechanic I. J. A. Francis (rigger), who were both mechanics based at Cranwell.

MacLaren was clearly very attached to Tiny, his Maltese terrier, who had already accompanied him and Amanda to Egypt when he was posted to 14 Squadron in 1915, so it was agreed that Tiny would accompany him on the flight to Egypt—the first dog ever to do so.

Dogs were a very important companion to pilots during the war, as they could offer a feeling of calm and safety at times of extreme fear. Maltese terriers were obedient and loved to be with people, and being small dogs were able to fit into the cockpit. Winston Churchill, when he was First Lord of the Admiralty, discussing their entry into the Naval Air Wing, had made the comment: 'We need not worry too much about educational tests. What is needed for this dangerous service is a young gentleman and a good animal.'[7] As MacLaren had not done well with his education at Charterhouse, but was a young gentleman with a good dog, it would seem that he could be thoroughly approved of in this context.

The route was planned by Borton and most of the airfields were known, certainly those from Cranwell to Otranto in Southern Italy, as they had already been used during the war and flown by Commander Savory in 1917. They were to start at Manston, Kent and from there fly to Paris, Lyon, Miramas, Pisa, Rome, Otranto, Crete, across the Mediterranean to Egypt, Matruh, Aboukir and finally Cairo. There was a seaplane base at Suda Bay in Crete, but as it had no airfield to land planes, a cable was sent to the Royal Navy in Malta requesting that a landing place be constructed and ready by 25 July. The Admiralty was also asked to provide two picket ships to escort them on the sea crossing to Egypt, just in case of any problems.

Arrangements were made for the dispatch of Castrol oil to be stored at all the proposed landing places, and other spares were selected in view of Commander Savory's previous experience. He had experienced considerable trouble with overheating and had carried a very large amount of spares on the machine, so travelling as light as possible was a major requirement. In turn, it was decided that non-essential spares could be dropped off at Otranto before making the sea crossing.

From 6 to 20 July, Borton and MacLaren spent a great deal of time at Cranwell supervising the fitting up of HP C9681, obtaining the spares required, and putting in as much flying time as possible to gain handling experience. The weather was mostly unfavourable during that time, but at least it gave them some idea of what they might expect during their journey.

They had a mascot called Marmaduke fixed on the front of the plane just behind the pilot's head, which had been given to them for 'good luck' by Borton's sister-in-law Lorna. This mascot was revered by MacLaren, who was to place it again on his plane when his adventurous soul flew in later years.

The flight itself was due to begin on 22 July but was a little delayed due to bad weather. They left for Manston, Kent shortly after 0700 on 24 July with Goldfinch and Francis but had more delays due to faulty magnetos and a problem with the port water pump. They finally reached Manston at 1020 on 25 July for a final inspection of the machine and its engines. This flight was regarded in the nature of a test, rather than an actual start of the journey, so that any modifications could be carried out at Manston. But fortunately, all previous calculations proved to be very satisfactory, meaning all was finally in order.

On 28 July 1918 everything was ready and they hoped to start off early on their way to Paris. But there was a strong wind and possibility of storms so they decided to wait until the afternoon. Then, at 1523, with the weather improving, the decision was made to set off. Borton's parents were at Manston, together with MacLaren's wife, Amanda, so that they could wave their farewells and see them off safely.

MacLaren was at the controls as they took off, as Borton decided to take on the duties of forward gunner in case of attack by enemy seaplanes. Luckily nothing untoward occurred, and they finally arrived at Villa Coublay Air Base in Paris (now with Borton at the controls) after a total distance of 100 miles and two hours and thirty-seven minutes of flying time. Both MacLaren and Borton shared the piloting throughout the flight to Cairo, which allowed them both to gain much flying experience as well as giving each of them some rest periods.

Borton and MacLaren (and Tiny) spent the night at the L'Hermitage Hotel, which was within a ten-minute walk of the aerodrome, but Goldfinch and Francis stayed with the machine as they would every night for the entire journey.

The following morning, 29 July, they set off early, at 0758, in hazy weather and flew along the Saône Valley to Lyon, landing at Fort Bron

Aerodrome at 1148. Photographs were taken of the route throughout the flight, although some did not come out due to fog and poor light. Upon their arrival, the commandant of the aerodrome gave them great assistance and petrol was readily supplied for refuelling.

A car was provided for Borton and MacLaren to go into Lyon for lunch, but as there was no accommodation to be had that night, they decided to stay in the aerodrome and sleep under the machine in an empty aeroplane case, which would allow them to be ready for another early start the next morning. Goldfinch and Francis slept inside the machine in order to keep guard. Borton wrote letters to his father at the family home at Cheveney in Kent, one of which mentioned an anecdote from Lyon:

> MacLaren's little 'Primus' was invaluable for a cup of cocoa which with biscuits and chocolate made an excellent breakfast at dawn... By 8.15pm we had finished our jobs, and in view of the fact that MacLaren's 'Primus' had tragically burst at tea time, we decided to go down to the station for dinner.[8]

So, on the morning of 30 July at 0657, they set off for Miramas Aerodrome in Marseilles. MacLaren was at the controls and Borton took over at 0820, reaching Miramas at 0910. This aerodrome was used as a large school for a considerable number of pupils, meaning they would be given great assistance. Having sent ahead vital stores in case of need, they found they had been well looked after.

A car was provided for Borton and MacLaren and they were given lunch at a buffet. They were then able to change the mahogany propeller for a walnut one, as it was experiencing engine revolutions that were too high. Also, the heat of the day had caused a tyre to burst, and so this too was replaced. Once again, they slept under the machine that night, despite Borton reporting that the 'dromo formed a somewhat nobbly couch, and the mosquitoes were most persistent and virulent'.[9]

After an early start at 0545 the following day, 31 July, in perfect weather, MacLaren went on to make 'a faultless landing under rather difficult conditions at the aerodrome' at Pisa, Italy at 1025.[10] As there were three aerodromes situated to the south of Pisa, it had been difficult to decide which to choose; they did in fact choose the one farthest from town, which was a bit of a mistake. However, they had the usual great assistance, and whilst there, they had to make a small repair to the fuselage where there had been a leak of acid from an accumulator. Once again, a car was placed at Borton and MacLaren's disposal (Goldfinch and Francis remaining with the plane), and they stayed overnight at the Hotel Minerva.

The following day, 1 August, they left at 0632 and made a very easy flight to Centocelle Airfield outside Rome, with MacLaren piloting the plane for the whole journey of two hours and forty-five minutes. Borton and MacLaren spent the afternoon sightseeing in Rome and once more slept under the machine in order to set off very early for Ortranto at 0440 the following morning, although they had been offered accommodation in the officer's quarters. MacLaren took charge of all the final preparations.

Their route took them past Naples, with MacLaren piloting while Borton took photographs of the city and the Mount Vesuvius crater. On passing Salerno, they found that their map was rather difficult to follow, so they kept within sight of the railway. Having earlier received news that the other British aerodrome north of Otranto had been abandoned, owing to an outbreak of malaria, they chose the airfield at Andrano, near Otranto, although it was a little smaller, where MacLaren made a faultless landing at 0950.

Here they decided to change the remaining three wheels, taking advantage of all the spares which were there, as they figured that the original tyres would have become strained by this stage of the journey. They also lightened the load on the plane as much as possible bearing in mind the next stage of the trip, which would be over sea in what was now very hot weather.

So, after two days of rest and Goldfinch having given the engine a good overhaul, they set off at 0435 on 4 August for Suda Bay Aerodrome in Crete. With the slight southerly breeze slowing before dawn, the weather was very hot, so they decided to head out to the sea for cooler air. The request for a new airfield to be prepared at Suda Bay from grazing land had been very satisfactorily achieved and was ready for their arrival.

Borton and MacLaren followed their usual procedure of taking turns at the controls, and although there was some anxiety regarding the journey, Borton was to report:

All further anxiety concerning the journey was here dispelled by Major MacLaren noticing, on the flat ground at the point, three drainage ditches each forming a perfect horse-shoe: a propitious omen.[11]

They landed at Suda Bay at 1050—their longest flight so far: 460 miles in six hours and fifteen minutes. As well as crossing the Sea of Crete, they also had to clear the tops of a mountain range; as they had no information from the maps as to how high these were, they flew at 9,000 ft, which was fortunately enough to surpass these obstacles.

They now had to wait for their destroyer escorts, HMS *Ribble* and HMS *Colne*, which were not available until noon on 6 August. However, taking off at that time would have meant flying in the heat of the day, so it was decided to delay their departure until 0415 on 7 August. This was a smooth flight, but due to crosswinds, they would alter course, meaning landfall would end up farther east than intended. Instead of arriving at Sollum on the African coast, they decided to land at Mersa Matruh (a port on the coast of Egypt), where they refuelled at 0925. MacLaren already knew this aerodrome and so made an easy landing. He then took off later in the day, at 1605, when it was cooler, and they completed the journey to Aboukir, the aerodrome for Alexandria; with Borton at the controls, they landed at 1820.

It was here they were met by the air officer commanding RAF Middle East, Major General Geoffrey Salmond, who had been in command of No. 5 Wing in the Middle East in 1915 and was known to both Borton and MacLaren.

It was suggested that Salmond would join them on the final leg to Cairo, to which he duly agreed. So, they set off on 8 August at 1633 for Cairo, and Salmond took over the controls for a short while, finally arriving at 1823 at the aerodrome of Heliopolis.

The whole journey had taken eleven days since leaving Manston, travelling 2,592 miles in thirty-six hours and thirty minutes at an average speed of 71 mph. The achievement of the longest distance flown in one journey at the time by Borton, MacLaren, Goldfinch and Francis was a prime example of an elusive combination of detailed planning, fine airmanship, almost ideal weather and just plain good luck. MacLaren and Borton were both awarded the Air Force Cross and the two mechanics, Goldfinch and Francis, received the Air Force Medal.

At the end of Borton's report of the journey, he was to note:

A separate report is being compiled by Major MacLaren on the arrangements necessary for the establishment of a Ferry Service of machines to the Middle East, and I am convinced that following the same, or a similar course, this should prove a perfectly simple and feasible undertaking which would have far-reaching results of the very greatest importance.

In conclusion I wish to place on record the valuable services rendered by Major MacLaren whose skill and judgement throughout, combined with his resource in all emergencies of the greatest assistance.[12]

There was no doubt that Tiny, MacLaren's Maltese terrier, had also gained a reputation as an aviator! He was always the first to leave the plane when they landed, no doubt because spending several hours on a cushion in the cabin with whoever was piloting became rather boring and a little frightening at times.

Borton was to write home from Palestine to his father, giving some amusing anecdotes about Tiny's experience:

Poor wee dog!... as soon as the engines were switched off, he announced that he wished to get down. The procedure was always the same... Tiny was handed out by the scruff of his neck... addressing the crowds at the top of his voice... However, he was always back at the foot of the ladder in time to sit up and beg as soon as either Mac's feet or mine appeared thro' the trapdoor.[13]

Having been fully overhauled, the Handley Page aircraft C9681 was now flown to Ramleh in Palestine to join No. 1 Squadron Australian

Flying Corp, where it was taken over by Captain Ross Smith in order to deliver large loads of fuel and ammunition to T. E. Lawrence's 'air base' in Azrak, Egypt.[14]

However, after some days of rest, it was noted on an army casualty form that MacLaren was now to return to 'Home Establishment' in the UK on the troopship HMS *Norman*, which left from Alexandria on 31 August.[15]

From now onwards, MacLaren was to get to know the Handley Page aircraft in much greater detail in the final stages of the First World War.

6

Second Flight to Egypt and First Flight to India

Archibald and Amanda's son Wallace was now seven months old, and on his return home Archibald was able to spend a little time enjoying being a father. The family were living in London but Amanda had been staying at Cheveney, Kent—the home of Biffy Borton—when she received a telegram from her husband in Rome saying 'Meet me Bonningtons Hotel London on Monday'.[1] They met in London and were both then asked back to Cheveney to share the amazing experience of the flight to Egypt and to show off MacLaren's Air Force Cross, which both pilots had been awarded.

However, barely two weeks had gone by when, at 1800 on 25 September 1918, MacLaren received a telegram instructing him to report immediately to the Air Ministry. The request was for him to repeat the journey to Egypt in another Handley Page 0/400, serial no. C9700, which had already seen active bombing service in France. He was ordered to proceed to Marseilles to take over the plane from Major Mansell and from there to proceed as quickly as possible to Egypt.

On 26 September, MacLaren first went to Hendon, where an Air DH.4 biplane had been ordered to stand by in readiness to take him to Paris. Leaving in very unsettled weather, he arrived at Le Bourget Aerodrome, Paris, at 1640, having landed twice to try and obtain petrol as his pilot thought they were running short. MacLaren then left on the overnight train to Marseilles and arrived the following morning. He then proceeded to the base commandant who put a car at his disposal in order to continue his journey to Miramas.

When MacLaren arrived, he was to find the plane in very bad condition. A recent mistral had blown the machine over onto one wing, causing considerable damage and burst tyres on all four wheels. Although much of the repair work had already been carried out in the shelter of a Bessoneaux hangar, MacLaren had to make sure the machine was safe for the journey, and that it was not overloaded for a long-distance flight. He therefore removed a double Lewis gun and also a number of full and empty drums from the front and rear gunners' cockpits, as well as an immense amount of what he considered to be unnecessary spares, chiefly wireless gear and accumulators. He then proceeded by car to the workshops and managed to persuade them to work all night to get everything ready for takeoff.

At 0920 on 28 September, MacLaren took off together with his co-pilot Lieutenant F. L. Hopps and two mechanics, 1st Air Mechanic Foster and 1st Air Mechanic Smith. A very strong wind was blowing from the north as they left, and it was decided that if they made good time, they should not land at Pisa but carry straight on to Rome. But MacLaren discovered that there was an air lock in the petrol pipe blocking the petrol flow, and they were therefore forced to descend in a large field near Grosseto, Italy to get the air lock out. However, after going a short distance, the same thing reoccurred, but this time they kept on and landed again on an Italian aerodrome at Cerveteri with five minutes petrol to spare.

They finally reached Rome at 1820, just as a thunderstorm was breaking. As it was too wet to be able to do any work to the machine, the mechanics were ordered to be up at dawn to carry on with the work. The machine was then covered up as much as possible to prevent the rain from falling into the cockpits. Then, after further work on the machine by the mechanics, they set off the following morning at 1150 for Salerno and once again encountered a great deal of bad weather until they reached Andrano aerodrome near the coastal town of Otranto. While they were here, two new wheels were fitted and they finally left at 1000 on 30 September in fine clear weather and a following wind, arriving at Suda Bay five hours later without incident.

Cables were dispatched to the Air Ministry to inform them of their safe arrival and their proposal to start the following morning for Egypt, weather permitting. However, a message was received from Cairo to the effect that they were not to start until further orders, so the following day was spent cleaning down the machine as well as giving the mechanics a day off. Then having received another message from Cairo stating that a start could be made if the weather was suitable, they set off at 0755 on 5 October and finally landed at Heliopolis at 1610.

MacLaren wrote a detailed report of the flight, which was sent to Major General W. Salmond, the general officer commanding RAF Middle East, the final paragraph of which read:

In conclusion I would like to add that I was met with the greatest courtesy at all stopping places, and that every help was given me during the journey. I cannot speak too highly of the valuable services rendered by Lieut. Hopps, and also those of 1st A.M. Foster and 1st A.M. Smith, the mechanics who accompanied us.[2]

In his reply to the Air Ministry, Salmond wrote:

I think this report shows that Major MacLaren acted with great promptitude and determination and would particularly draw your attention to the speed with which he accomplished the journey. His flights from Marseilles to Rome and from Crete to Cairo without a stop, are noteworthy achievements. I consider great credit is due to Major MacLaren.[3]

Having already been awarded the Air Force Cross for co-piloting the first flight to Egypt, MacLaren should have been granted a bar to the AFC, but this seemed to have been overlooked.

MacLaren then returned to England and was once again requested to pilot another Handley Page aircraft. This would be for the first through flight from England to India; the machine chosen this time was a V/1500, serial no. J1936. MacLaren selected a route to Egypt that he had already followed, and from there would go on to Palestine, Mesopotamia, the north side of the Persian Gulf and finally Karachi, then part of the British Indian Empire.

This huge machine was powered by two pairs of 375-hp Rolls Royce Eagle VIII engines and had almost double the wingspan of the 0/400 with a cruising speed of 85 mph. It had originally been designed and built to bomb Berlin from bases in East Anglia, but the armistice was declared before it had become operational. Now the interior was built so that it could be fitted with seats for passengers instead of racks for bombs. It measured 127 ft from wing-tip to wing-tip, and the weight with fuel and passengers was about 27,000 lbs.

MacLaren chose Captain Robert 'Jock' Halley DFC AFC as his co-pilot for this flight, as he already had some experience flying this type of aircraft as a long-distance bomber pilot and had been with the Independent Air Force (IAF) in France from the time it was formed in June 1918 until it was disbanded at the end of the First World War. There were three other crew members: Flight Sergeant Albert Edward Smith and Sergeant William Crockett, both fitters, and Sergeant Thomas Brown, a rigger. They were also to take one passenger— Brigadier General Norman Duckworth Kerr MacEwen CB CMG DSO RAF—who had been appointed to command the RAF in India. The name of the aircraft, painted on the nose of the plane, was 'His Majesty's Airship (HMA) *Old Carthusian*', as both MacLaren and MacEwen had been educated at Charterhouse School.

Captain Halley was also to mention:

MacLaren and I had a lot in common, except that he was 6ft. 2in. and I 5ft. 3in. wearing my thick socks! He was also a Scot and had already flown to Egypt in an 0/400 with General 'Biffy' Borton. Our considerable experience on heavy aircraft had brought us together.[4]

MacLaren's wife Amanda was among the little party gathered to give the voyagers God-speed and perched on the hump of the fuselage was a small brown-and-white curly toy dog placed there as a mascot in memory of MacLaren's dog Tiny, who had travelled with him on his first flight to Egypt and would be joining them again in Paris.

The *Old Carthusian* took off from the RAF Station at Martlesham Heath, Suffolk at 0942 on 8 December 1918 in fine weather but, due to problems with the starboard engine's reduction gear, was forced to return soon afterwards. It took the Rolls Royce mechanics five days to fit new gears to the engines; they set off again at 0945 on 13 December, when the weather had cleared enough and there was a strong westerly wind. Just after leaving the ground, one of the manifolds of the starboard rear engine broke at the joint, and for a moment it was thought that they would again have to land. But as the bracket appeared to be holding satisfactorily and the part which had come adrift was acting as a shield between the actual exhaust and the engine, it was decided to proceed.

Heading over the Channel, and despite the good weather conditions at Martlesham, they flew into dense cloud and rainstorms over France. MacLaren decided to search for somewhere to land, and at 1250 they touched down at Bergues Aerodrome near Dunkirk, where they spent the night.

In Brigadier General MacEwen's later report, he was very complimentary of MacLaren's piloting: 'Major MacLaren piloted the machine during the whole of this flight and his handling of it, under most difficult weather conditions, was excellent in every way.'[5]

The next day they flew on to Le Bourget, Paris, where they landed at 1205. Here MacLaren was joined once again by his dear little Maltese terrier Tiny, whom he had left with friends in Paris under British quarantine rules on his return from Egypt a few weeks earlier. MacLaren claimed that with 170 flying hours Tiny was the world's most air-travelled dog, and there was no doubt that he was thrilled to run up into the cockpit once again.[6]

They were now very surprised to find that an account of their proposed journey to India had appeared in the Paris *Daily Mail* on the morning of 14 December. They were at a loss to understand how this information had been obtained, as they had been instructed by the Air Ministry that the trip was supposed to be kept secret.[7]

They left Le Bourget on 15 December, making two forced landings at Beaune, France and Pisa, Italy due to bad weather, and then flew on down the Italian coast to Sicily. They had planned to fly from Rome to Athens on 19 December, but this had to be changed as they realised that the *Old Carthusian* would not clear the Apennine mountains safely. So, it was decided to follow the route around the toe of Italy, and as the weather was still bad and the turbulence very severe, it took both pilots on the controls to keep the plane steady at 200 ft.

Finally, they arrived at the aerodrome at Catania, Sicily at 1527. They decided to land there as fuel was running low. Fortunately, while they had been in Rome, MacLaren had obtained a map from the Italians, and this showed them where the aerodrome was situated. But landing was not as easy as expected. The ground being soft and boggy, their wheels sank in up to the axles. MacLaren somehow prevented her from going onto her nose. It then took a team of 100 soldiers from the Sicilian army, led by a general, to help dig her out.

They finally took off for Malta on 21 December and landed at the Marsa sports ground, the only flat piece of land that could accommodate an aircraft the size of the *Old Carthusian*. They managed to fill up with some British Aviation petrol, and then took off again at 0200 the following day, narrowly missing a stone wall before beginning a steady climb on the 1,150-mile journey to Cairo.

They planned to land at Benghazi, in north-eastern Libya. But at 0925 the rear engine failed, so they made the decision to stop off at Alexandra. Then the other starboard engine failed as well, and Halley made an emergency landing on flat scrub about 50 miles west of Mersa Matruh, Egypt. It turned out that the engine failures had been caused by broken reduction gears, and to top it all two tyres were punctured on landing.

Fortunately, some Arabs miraculously appeared soon after they landed, and with the promise of a payment of gold sovereigns—which luckily MacEwen had managed to obtain from the treasury back in England, just in case they would prove useful—the Arabs left to get assistance. The crew spent the night under the plane's wings and inside the fuselage, which was very uncomfortable, especially as the temperature dropped.

Help arrived the following morning, and the crew travelled by rail and road to Cairo, where they stayed at the Shepheard's Hotel for some festive Christmas celebrations. By 29 December a team of RAF ground crew arrived from Aboukir bringing the necessary spare parts. Repairs were achieved by Smith, Crockett and Brown with the help of the RAF team and at 1300 on 31 December the *Old Carthusian* took off once again for Heliopolis, Cairo, where she was given a thorough overhaul.

They departed from Heliopolis at 0330 on 8 January 1919 with the intention of flying non-stop to Ahwaz, Persia, but once again they encountered problems with all of the engines, until the revolution counters were 'doing a kind of clog dance' according to MacLaren.[8] Disappointed, they were forced to land at Abu Kamal, near the Euphrates, at 1400, where they cleaned out all the filters in the engines and set off once again at 1515. After another overnight landing, due to strong headwinds and an approaching storm, they finally arrived in the Iraqi capital the following morning.

Three days were spent in Baghdad repairing propellers, which had been damaged by metal blown off the petrol-pump wind-vane cups. They set off towards Bushire on 11 January, accompanied by an SE5A biplane and a Bristol monoplane for forty-five minutes.

A stop was made at the Persian city of Ahwaz, where yet more repairs were made, and then they flew on to Bushire, racing across the desert at very low heights of between 10 and 100 ft. Sunday 12 of January saw them achieve the next leg to Bandar Abbas. They then flew on to Karachi the following day, despite the crew feeling that the engines should be given another overhaul, which was to prove right. They once again had to make an emergency landing after leaving Bandar Abbas, as the port rear engine seized while crossing the Arabian Sea. MacLaren turned inland and they arrived safely on a long spit of sand near Ormara, a fishing village 170 miles west of Karachi.

There had been so many unfortunate delays already on this flight out to India that MacLaren was now very keen to continue as quickly as possible. The decisions of what to do had now to be made. MacEwen thought that if the machine continued to be subjected to the exposure of the climate, the wooden structure would not be able to sustain it and they would have to dismantle *Old Carthusian* and ship her back to England, which would destroy the whole hope of reaching India by air. However, MacLaren thought there was the possibility that they could attempt to fly out with just three engines.

As luck would have it, a number of people had come to witness their arrival, one being an immensely helpful Indian official of the

Eastern Telegraph Company, who sent out messages for assistance and organised accommodation for the crew. Much work was now done by the fitters on the three good engines, and they also set about attempting to reduce the weight of the aircraft by stripping off all surplus items and only taking on the 220 gallons of fuel to get them to Karachi.

During this time, there had been many cables sent to and from Karachi explaining the situation. Brigadier General MacEwen had been suffering from heat exhaustion and was not at all well, so the Royal Indian Navy sent an old gunboat, HMS *Britomart*, from Karachi to take MacEwen aboard as he was already late for his new appointment of command in India. In order to offload as much weight as possible from the aircraft, they also loaded all their heavy baggage onto the *Britomart*, which was soon on its way back to Karachi.

One other decision taken by MacLaren and Halley was that, in order to take the most weight off the plane to allow for the best takeoff, only Flight Sergeant Smith would remain with them, and would sit in the rear cockpit for ultimate balance.

But this was not to be the end of the problems with the engines. MacLaren took off successfully as he taxied his way between the sand dunes at 1745 and reached 1,000 ft as they were passing the *Britomart* on their starboard side. But then the two starboard engines came to grief and stopped. The conclusion was that the main wind-driven pump had failed to feed petrol to the engines, but with immense determination Halley and Smith worked hard to control this with an emergency hand pump.

It was now 1845 and dark, and with 35 miles still to go until Karachi, they realised there was yet another problem: the rear engine had started to overheat and now needed to be shut down. The crew just hoped they could hold out with only the remaining two engines on each side of the plane.

As they began to lose height over the next 30 minutes, MacLaren managed to hold the speed at 52 mph, until fortunately they noticed a flarepath made from petrol-soaked rags laid down by the royal engineers in Karachi. As luck would have it, they had been earlier notified by Sergeant Brown in Ormara and had rushed to be of help.

So, at 1915 on 15 January 1919, the *Old Carthusian* safely touched down at her final destination. This epic flight had covered 5,560 miles since leaving England in a flying time of seventy-two hours and forty-one minutes, at an average speed of 77 mph.

There was no doubt that there had been many mechanical problems during their flight in the Handley Page V1500 aeroplane. Having been the main pilot, MacLaren took it upon himself to write a very detailed report to outline his reasoning in regard to its behaviour and its suitability for this type of work.

Criticisms on the V1500 type Handley Page aeroplane

Having had a certain amount of practical experience on the V1500 type Handley Page in connection of long distance flights, I venture to make a few criticisms in regard to its behaviour and its suitability for this type of work.

In the first place I am convinced that the machine is under-engined, as I found that with a moderate load (approx. weight of machine 16,000 lbs and approx. weight of fuel, baggage, including spares and personnel 6,500 lbs. Total 22,500 or possibly 23,000 lbs.) at a height of 5,000 feet, it was necessary for me to run the rear engines at a speed of 1,675 revs. per minute and the front ones at a speed of 1600 revs. per minute, at a cruising speed of 80 M.P.H., in order to prevent the machine from losing height. Similarly whilst crossing the Mediterranean at a height of 2,000 feet with a total load of approx. 26,000 or 26,500 lbs, the rear engines had to be run at 1,700 revs. per minute and the front ones at almost 1,650 revs. per minute, at a cruising speed of 80 M.P.H. In this latter case all throttles had to be nearly wide open, this being due to the fact that the quality of Italian aviation petrol was so inferior as to cause the loss of almost 75 revs. per minute per engine, although in the case of the Mediterranean run, the tanks were more than half full of British Aviation petrol which had been added to the Italian petrol, as there was no time to empty the Italian petrol out on arrival at Malta.

Whilst endeavouring to cross the Italian mountains, I found it impossible to climb the machine above 7,000 feet, even lightly loaded as she was. This may be partly due to the fact that the machine may have lost a certain amount of incidence during the flight out, although at this juncture it is impossible to say for certain, as the incidence of the main planes on departure was unknown to me. Furthermore, I have found that even with a slight breeze and a load of 26,000 lbs it has been impossible to lift the machine off the ground under a run of 800 yards, thus necessitating the use of large aerodromes throughout the route. As regards the landing speed, this is very fair for a machine of such dimensions, although if heavily loaded, it will drop if brought down at anything under 70 M.P.H.

The undercarriage appears to me to be excellent and very strong, for, whilst at Catania in Sicily, the soggy condition and the nature of the aerodrome necessitated my getting off partially down wind and very much cross-wind in a strong wind, and on examination of the undercarriage at the next aerodrome, no undue strain seems to have occurred at any point. Similarly, during a forced landing in the desert between Sollum and Matruh, the undercarriage was subjected to very heavy strains, due to the stony and very uneven nature of the ground, but again appears to be no worse for it. I have had a great deal of trouble with the inter-bracing wires of the tail plane, these having broken time and again, due to the heavy strains imposed upon the empennage due to the weather, of which I have had a considerable amount during the flight.

I am therefore having all inter-bracing wires of a larger gauge fitted, and recommend that all other machines of this type be fitted similarly. Lastly, as regards the machine, I would urge that more attention be paid to the fittings on the machine such as Radiator shutters and levers, Altitude control levers, and the necessity of considering the comfort of the pilot, as such small items as these make a vast amount of difference in the running and upkeep of the machine.

The fewer the worries of the pilot, the more the efficiency of both pilot and machine and if a pilot has continually to be wondering if his radiator shutter will open or close properly, or tying up his altitude control levers with bits of string to prevent them from opening themselves, it is obvious that he cannot pay so much attention to his other work, consequently, less efficiency all round.

Furthermore, I would like to add a few words about the engines themselves:

There is no doubt that the engines have been overtaxed during the whole flight, but have responded nobly to the demands put upon them, <u>but</u> there is one fault that must be investigated and rectified immediately. This is the continual breaking of the sun-wheel carrier in the reduction gear of the Rolls Royce Eagle VIII engines.

Since the commencement of this flight, I have had three breaks. The first one ten minutes after leaving Martlesham Heath, and the other two within one hour of each other along the North African Coast. I can only account for their breaking, as being due to the machine either being overloaded or under-engined, or else faulty material being used in the manufacture. In my opinion, in these three cases, the fault has been due to the machine being under-engined, consequently overloading the engines. Especially would it be so in the case of the third breakage, as the machine was then flying on three engines, consequently the strain on the single one must have been enormous.

In conclusion I would like to add that, taking into consideration the conditions appertaining during this time of the year, the machine has, on the whole, behaved extremely well, but is very heavy on controls, both fore and aft, but more especially lateral, and in very bumpy weather required the use of two pairs of hands to keep the machine under control. A little more balance on the ailerons I feel sure would help matters a lot.

Signed: A. Stuart MacLaren—Major
Dated: 4/1/19 Cairo[9]

Captain Halley was awarded an Air Force Cross (AFC) and Smith, Crockett and Brown all received the Air Force Medal. Brigadier General McEwen wrote to the Air Ministry saying that he could not speak too highly of their enterprise, grit and determination for successfully completing the flight in the face of so many difficulties.[10]

The No. 1 Aerial Route

The RAF was considerably reduced in size following the end of the First World War, and the only immediate requirement for military force was now in the colonies.

There was still considerable unrest in Egypt, and it was understood that the RAF could provide Handley Page o/400 bombers to assist with the fighting in the desert. Though there were many currently in France, which could be packed into crates, sent by rail to Marseille and shipped to Alexandria, where they would be reassembled in the RAF aeroplane factory in Heliopolis, this would take time and the planes were needed urgently. And although a factory had already been built in Heliopolis, it could only build fighter aeroplanes, not bombers.

On 28 August, a letter from Major General Geoffrey Salmond, then commanding the RAF in the Middle East, was dispatched to the chief of the air staff, Major General Sir Frederick Sykes, suggesting that an aerial route between England, Italy and the Middle East would be the best way of ferrying planes out at this time. He explained:

This route would be capable of supplying the Royal Air Force Units in the following places:

ITALY – OTRANTO – SALONIKA (Greece) – EGYPT
The saving in shipping and railway traffic would be very large indeed, and this is particularly the case as regards Egypt where the demand for service types of machines both for training and for operations will require fully 45 of these service machines per month.

The MacLaren family—Ethel, John Wallace and their two sons, Cecil and Archie. (*Time To Spare? A History of Summer Fields*)

The portrait of Ethel McLaren at Summer Fields School. (*Time To Spare? A History of Summer Fields*)

Above: Ethel and Archie riding 'Scarlet Runner' on the Schatzlap Run in Davos. (*MacLaren family photo*)

Left: Archie. (*MacLaren family photo*)

Archie during his days at Charterhouse School. (*MacLaren family photo*)

Violet Emily Dimble. (*MacLaren family photo*)

Amanda and Archibald Stuart-MacLaren. (*MacLaren family photo*)

The Royal Flying Corps recruitment poster. (*Army Flying Museum, Hampshire*)

1310

MACLAREN, Archibald Stuart Charles Stuart-
    Headquarters, Royal Flying Corps,
            South Farnborough, Hants.

Born 15th May, 1892.   at Whitchurch, Oxon
Nationality British
Rank or Profession 2nd Air Mechanic

Certificate taken on Caudron Biplane
At British Flying School, Le Crotoy, France
Date 4th June, 1915.
Duplicate handed in 19. 4. 20

Above: Royal Aero Club certificate number 1310. (*The National Archives, London*)

Left: MacLaren: gazetted flying officer of the RFC. (*MacLaren family photo*)

Right: Archibald and
Amanda at Heliopolis.
(*MacLaren family photo*)

Below: Archibald, Amanda
and Tiny at Ismailia.
(*MacLaren family photo*)

Left: Second Lieutenant MacLaren and Captain Blackburn. (*Michael Hallett, grandson of Captain Blackburn*)

Below: De Havilland Airco DH.1A biplane. (*Grace's Guide to British Industrial History*)

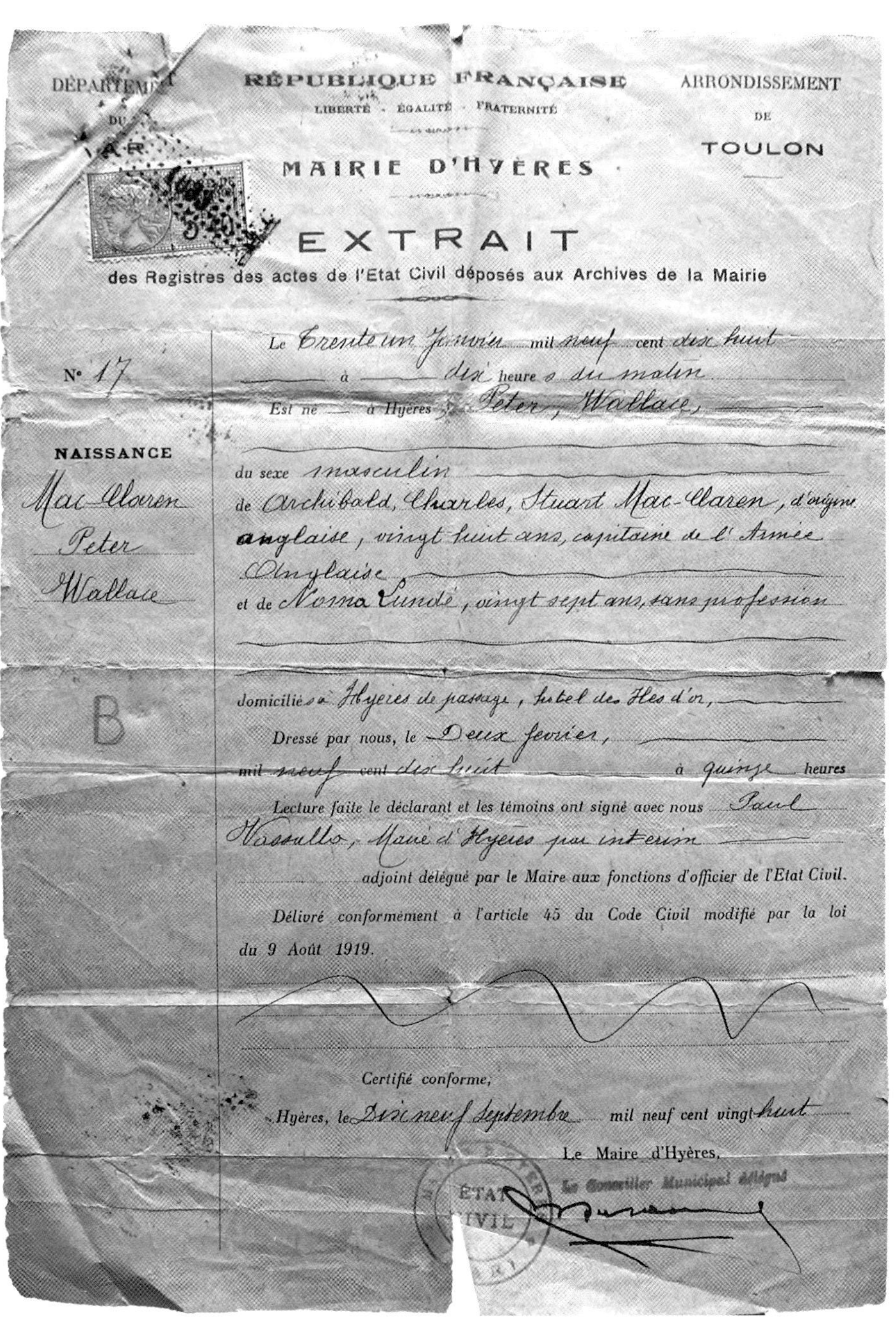

French birth certificate for Geoffrey Wallace Peter Stuart-MacLaren. (*MacLaren family photo*)

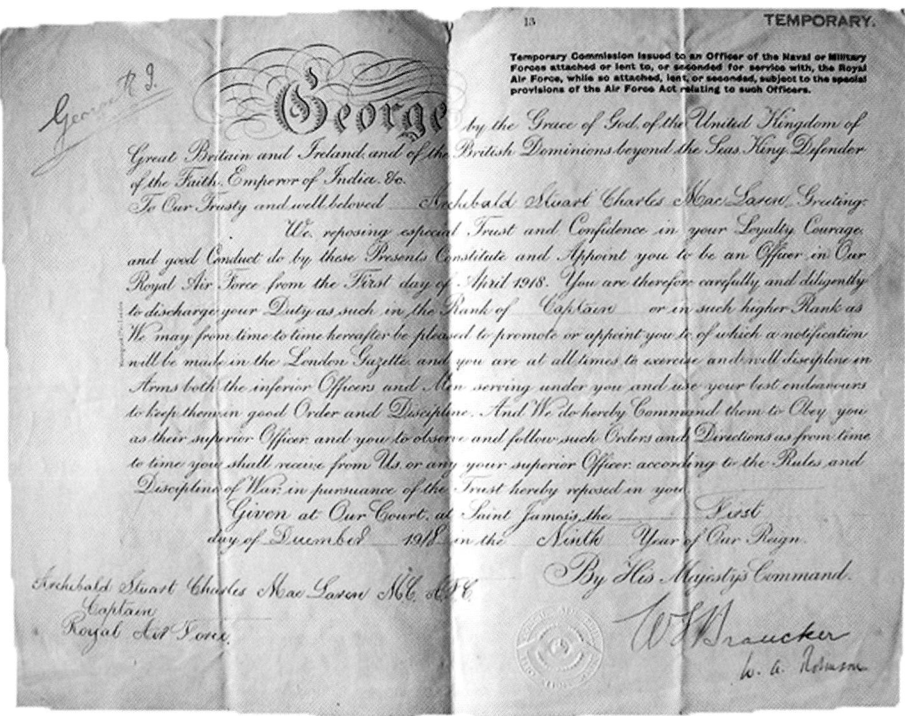

13

TEMPORARY.

Temporary Commission issued to an Officer of the Naval or Military Forces attached or lent to, or seconded for service with, the Royal Air Force, while so attached, lent, or seconded, subject to the special provisions of the Air Force Act relating to such Officers.

George R.I.

George by the Grace of God, of the United Kingdom of Great Britain and Ireland and of the British Dominions beyond the Seas King, Defender of the Faith, Emperor of India, &c.

To Our Trusty and well beloved _Archibald Stuart Charles MacLaren_ Greeting:

We, reposing especial Trust and Confidence in your Loyalty, Courage, and good Conduct do by these Presents Constitute and Appoint you to be an Officer in Our Royal Air Force from the First day of April 1918. You are therefore carefully and diligently to discharge your Duty as such in the Rank of _Captain_ or in such higher Rank as We may from time to time hereafter be pleased to promote or appoint you to, of which a notification will be made in the London Gazette, and you are at all times to exercise and well discipline in Arms both the inferior Officers and Men serving under you and use your best endeavours to keep them in good Order and Discipline. And We do hereby Command them to Obey you as their superior Officer and you to observe and follow such Orders and Directions as from time to time you shall receive from Us, or any your superior Officer, according to the Rules and Discipline of War, in pursuance of the Trust hereby reposed in you.

Given at Our Court, at Saint James's, the _First_ day of _December_ 1918 in the _Ninth_ Year of Our Reign.

By His Majesty's Command.

W. S. Braucker
W. A. Robinson

Archibald Stuart Charles MacLaren MC AFC
Captain
Royal Air Force.

MacLaren's RAF commission—service number 2663, 1918. (*MacLaren family*)

Handley Page 0/400 C9681 with the crew, including Tiny. (*The National Archives AIR1/913/204/5/854*)

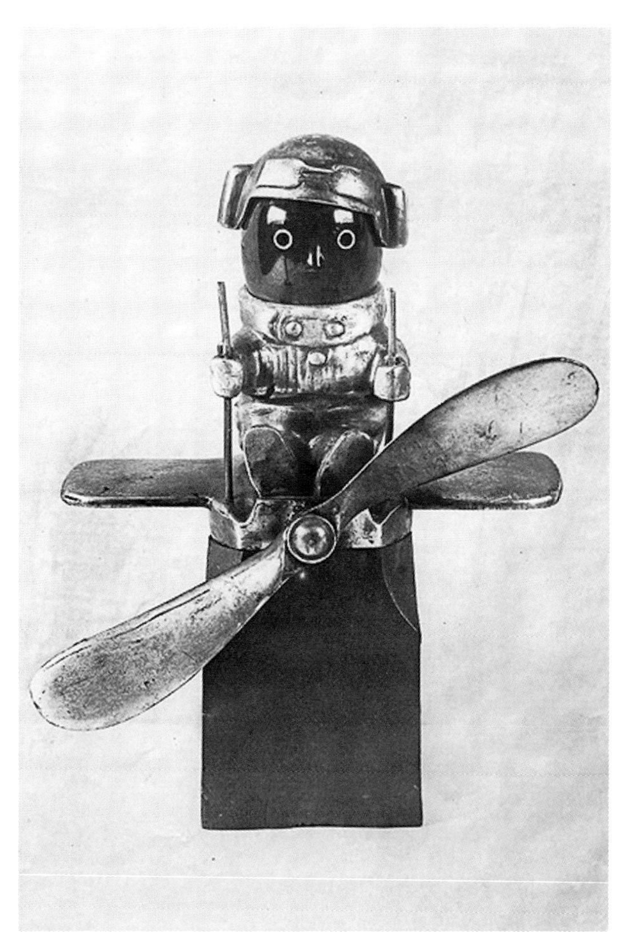

Right: Lucky mascot
Marmaduke. (*MacLaren
family photo*)

Below: Handley Page 0/400
C9681. (*The National
Museum of the Royal Navy*)

Left: Tiny, the Maltese terrier. (*MacLaren family photo*)

Below: Handley Page V/1500 heavy bomber *Old Carthusian*, India, March 1919. (*Air Historical branch RAF*)

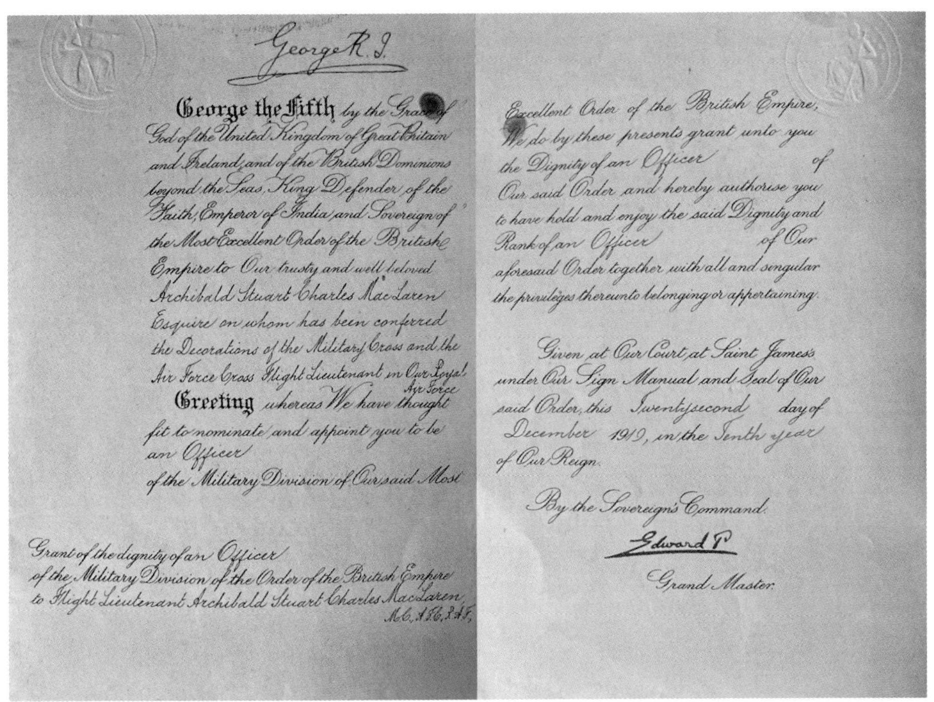

OBE. (*MacLaren family*)

The name 'Old Carthusian 11' being painted on the nose of the HP 0/400. (*MacLaren family photo*)

Left: Flying Officer William Noble Plenderleith. (*Shelley Wilkes (née Plenderleith*))

Below: Sergeant William Herbert Andrews. (*Shelley Wilkes (née Plenderleith*))

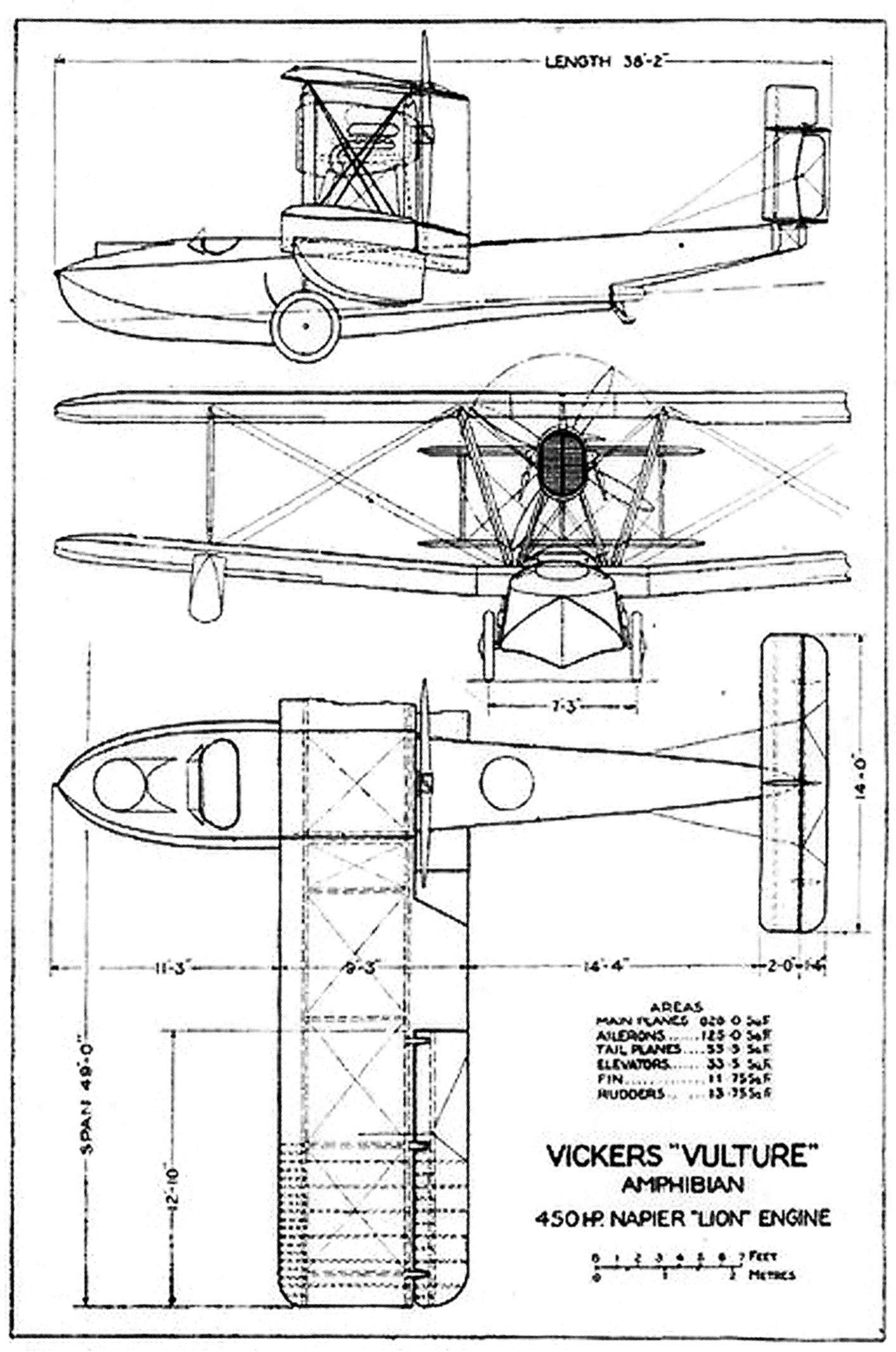

Drawing of the Vickers Vulture aeroplane. (Flight, *27 March 1924*)

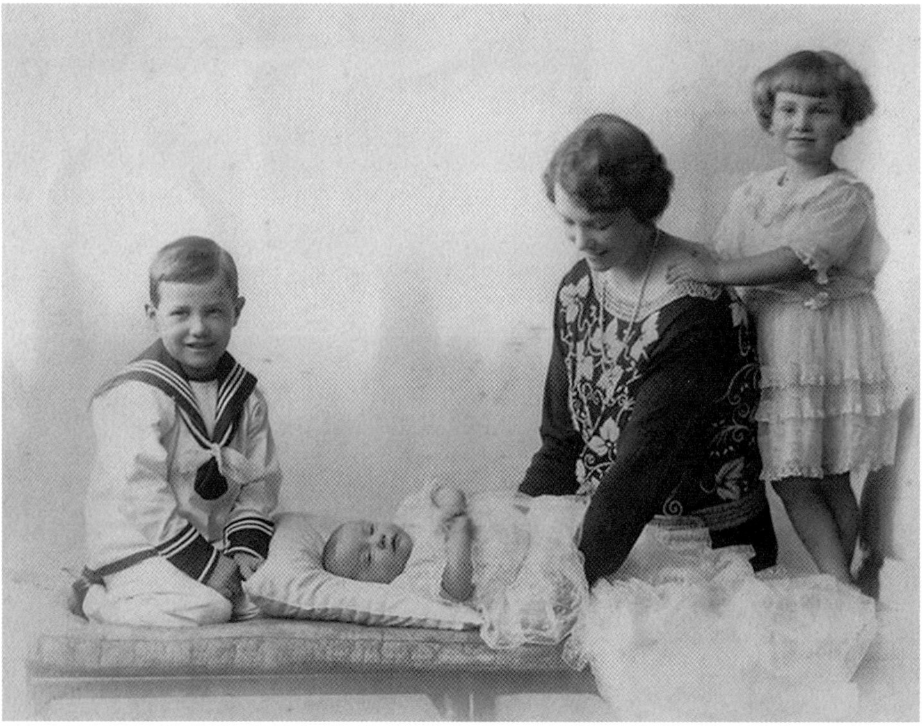

Amanda with Wallace, Anna and baby Hugh. (*MacLaren family photo*)

Vickers Vulture G-EBHO. (*RAF Museum—Hendon*)

At the same time acceptance work would be greatly reduced at all the stations since erection work for all these types would no longer be necessary and this would result in a corresponding decrease in establishments....... I very strongly recommend that Major A. S. C. MacLaren should be at once detailed to organise this line of communication, since he has had experience of the route himself and has also had the necessary initiative to work it out in detail.[1]

After their groundbreaking flight in the *Old Carthusian*, MacLaren now returned to England towards the end of February 1919 to establish what was to be called 'No. 1 Aerial Route RAF.' Although this plan was not welcomed by everyone in the Air Ministry, especially since the drastic post-war expenditure cuts, it was nevertheless decided that it should go ahead.

Major General Salmond estimated it would take six days to fly a Handley Page aircraft to Cairo, rather than approximately four weeks to ship it out, and the route was now placed under the command of Major MacLaren, O.C. No. 1 Aerial Route RAF, based at St Raphael near Marseille. MacLaren started issuing orders for route station commanders (London to Cairo): 'The main object of the route is primarily for the dispatch of aeroplanes from England to Egypt, and secondly for assistance of such aeroplanes as may require from time to time to traverse this route on duty...'[2]

He then mapped out all instructions for each possible eventuality as well as the telegraphic addresses along the way. These were given alphabetic letters from A to J.[3] The pages also listed all the responsibilities of those personnel posted to the route. At that time the staffing of some of the smaller airfields was fairly nominal and had only a rigger and two fitters for refuelling and minor repairs, with a non-commissioned officer in charge. The larger stations had many more and one of the officers had to be a Handley Page pilot. Their responsibilities were to be involved with refuelling and maintenance of stocks of petrol and lubricants, upkeep and maintenance of the machines, arranging for the supply of spares, providing meals and accommodation for air crews en route, providing weather forecasts and notifying MacLaren at the St Raphael headquarters of each machine's progress.

In the case of any forced landings along the way, MacLaren wrote:

> [...] pilots will be instructed to telephone or telegraph to their nearest station, giving the exact position of their machine and the cause of their landing together with a list of the spares required to make the machine serviceable. Two mechanics will at once be sent down by passenger train or the quickest available means with the necessary spares. Should the ground be unsuitable i.e.: for taking off, the local authorities will be approached with a view to helping to transport the machine to some suitable ground in the vicinity, and failing this, or in the event of the machine being too much damaged to take off, the machine will have to be dismantled and taken to the nearest aerodrome by rail or road.[4]

The general scheme was now designed as follows:

Lympne to Paris
Paris to Lyons
Lyons to Marseilles
Marseilles to Genoa
Genoa to Rome
Rome to Foggia
Foggia to Otranto
Otranto to Kourtessi
Kourtessi to Suda Bay
Suda Bay to Sollum
Sollum to Alexandria

As the months went on, there were a great deal of problems due to delays, weather conditions, illness, lack of staff in some of the route stops, concern for some of the men's safety and sadly the loss of some pilots in crashes partly due to what was seen by some as MacLaren's lack of proper preparation of the route. True to character, MacLaren—strict disciplinarian that he was—wanted to get on with pushing the aeroplanes along to their destination as fast as possible, as this was also what Major General Salmond had ordered him to do.

By May 1919 concern was growing at the Air Ministry about a lack of proper management and control of the air route. It was considered that more staff were needed to man the route stations, and the aeroplanes required more spares. On 20 June MacLaren complained to the Air Ministry that mail arriving by the military airmail service was taking three weeks, whereas the civil post took only three days. He also complained that the proposal to base seaplanes at Taranto was nonsense because the longest over-sea flight between there and Suda Bay was only fifty miles. They were needed at Suda Bay for the 400-mile leg to Mersah Matruh.

Then came the bad news that the seaplane base at Suda Bay would be closed down at the end of July as part of the post-war economies. Many changes were made to attempt to dissipate the growing problems. By July, the Air Ministry began recruiting pilots back in England for the twenty-four extra aeroplanes they now planned to send to France, but all this was taking time and MacLaren was concerned with the lack of support he was receiving from the navy, the Air Ministry and the Army Ordnance Corps (AOC) Middle East.

At the beginning of September, there were further crashes, destroying more Handley Page aircraft as well as a Vickers Vimy, which crashed and caught fire near Bracciano, Italy killing the pilot. MacLaren was very disheartened by all this and was to explain to his boss, General P. W. Game, director of training and organisation at the Air Ministry, that he considered No. 1 Aerial Route to have been a complete failure, despite putting his heart and soul into it.

By November, MacLaren had moved his headquarters from St Raphael to Taranto, Italy, as he believed this was a better place for him to control the most difficult part of the route. However, the Air Ministry was now pressing him to acknowledge that there was too much risk involved in trying to fly the machines on the aerial route, and to once again consider sending the Handley Pages by sea, thus cutting out the loss of machine and life, which had happened so many times already.

MacLaren was then informed by General Game that he was to be relieved of his duties and must attend a court of enquiry at the Air Ministry in London ordered by Air Marshal Hugh Trenchard, chief of the air staff.

Before he left, MacLaren wrote a detailed report to the Air Ministry outlining all the crashes which had occurred to machines passing through No. 1 Aerial Route together with a summary of the many criticisms, which may have been of use to the court. He concluded by saying that the chief reason for the crashes, in his opinion, were due to errors of judgement by the pilots, faulty petrol systems, prevailing elements and lack of hanger accommodation.

Squadron Leader A. M. Wilson MBE was ordered to take over from MacLaren, and General Game sent a letter to him in Paris on 31 October 1919 instructing him to proceed straightaway to the St Raphael headquarters, where he was to begin the disbandment of No. 1 Aerial Route as rapidly as possible and retain command of the whole route until all the machines had arrived in Egypt.

On 13 November, MacLaren left Taranto for St Raphael and then on to London to attend the court of enquiry. Despite MacLaren's feeling that No. 1 Aerial Route had been a complete failure, all the evidence and criticisms put forward led to the decision that he was not personally to blame and was thus exonerated. From the grave allegations that were gathered and the conclusions of the investigating committee, a great deal of experience and knowledge had been gained.

8

Work in the Middle East

MacLaren returned home to spend a short time with his family, and then on 28 November 1919 was requested to return to Egypt—somewhere he was very familiar with—to be flight commander of 216 Squadron. This squadron had been involved in strategic bombing operations using Handley Page 0/400 heavy bombers in France in the First World War, but after being moved to El Kantara on the Suez Canal and equipped with Bristol Fighters (or 'Brisfits' as they were popularly known), it was now transporting mail and passengers throughout the Middle East.[1]

While MacLaren was in El Kantara, there came a notice from St James's Palace on 22 December 1919, confirming his OBE:

The KING has been graciously pleased to give orders for the following appointment to the Most Excellent Order of the British Empire, in recognition of distinguished services rendered during the War:

RAF—Fight Lieutenant Archibald Stuart Charles MacLaren O.B.E., M.C., A.F.C.[2]

Once again he had been acknowledged and well rewarded for his outright bravery in the Middle East during the First World War, having flown a total of 1,500 hours , no mean feat.

While MacLaren was away in Egypt, his wife Amanda gave birth in Paddington, London to their second child, a daughter, Lillian Anna (known as Anna). Amanda made some brief visits to Egypt with both

Wallace and Anna while her husband was posted there, so that he was able to keep in touch and watch them growing.

MacLaren was moved around Egypt during the next two years so that his expertise could be used where it was needed. But on 4 March 1920 he was back in England being entertained at a luncheon at the House of Commons together with Flight Sergeant Albert Smith, Sergeant William Crockett and Sergeant Thomas Brown, the *Old Carthusian* crew who had flown with MacLaren from England to India back in 1918. This was hosted by The Right Honourable John Seely, MP and Mr Clement Edwards, MP in commemoration of their great achievement.

MacLaren's 'sense of adventure' then saw him then entering the *Daily Express* £10,000 prize Air Cargo Race from England to India and back, starting from the Waddon Aerodrome, Croyden. The first two competitors—Major MacLaren accompanied by Captain J. A. Barton as navigating officer—would leave on Saturday 15 May in a Handley Page aircraft o/400 called *Old Carthusian II*. Captain Barton, a member of the RAF Club, had also flown a great number of miles. In 1915, he had been sent to Egypt with MacLaren and often acted at that time as his observer; they had also been close friends for many years.

The other two competitors—Mr R.W. Kenworthy accompanied by Captain C. H. Wilkins MC as navigating officer—set off in a Blackburn Kangaroo fighting bomber a few days later. It was obviously necessary, in the absence of government support, that steps should be taken to lend the strongest encouragement to the development of a reliable flight for commercial purposes.

Mr Frederick Handley Page was to nominate MacLaren as one of the best pilots in the opinion of the firm. The *Daily Express* explained the reason for this race:

The object of this competition is clear and practical. The idea is not to encourage any sensationalism in the air, but to prove that aviation is the 'transport of the future'. The "Daily Express" seeks to establish a usefulness in commerce which has been abundantly proved in war, to demonstrate the capacity of the modern aeroplane for work less murderous than bombing [...]. Saturday will be a red-letter day in the history of flying, for no competition affording so thorough and practical a test of the aeroplane's commercial capabilities and offering such encouragement to designers and builders of machines intended for commercial use has yet taken place. The race will also be a great sporting event—a supreme test of skill and grit—and will be followed with enthralled interest by the whole world.[3]

The conditions of the flight required the competitors to carry a cargo of 1,200 lbs from England to India and back. The time occupied on either the outward or the homeward journey was not to exceed 288 hours, and the return flight had to begin within fifteen days of arriving in India.

Unfortunately, this race would never take place, as the Air Ministry contacted the paper to explain that, owing to disturbances in Syria and Arabia, flying over those countries was dangerous, and the airmen would not be permitted to cross on the Athens-Suda Bay-Cairo route.

As can be imagined, MacLaren was most disappointed and in an interview with the *Daily Express* said:

It certainly is rough luck. Everything was ready and in perfect order. The chief reason that I am sorry for the delay is that I had fixed this date so that meteorological conditions would favour us. I had hoped to avoid the monsoons... my wife was to have flown with me from Cricklewood to Waddon tomorrow, but as the flight is postponed I shall take her for a flight over London.

Once more required to return to Egypt and on 9 September 1920, MacLaren is listed in the air force lists as supernumerary, RAF depot (in transit from Middle East). This means that he was given a variety of jobs before being seconded to join 208 Squadron RAF, which, having been based in France for the last two years, reformed on 1 February 1920 at RAF Ismailia in Egypt as a general purpose unit. Their motto was 'Vigilant'.

The squadron served in the Middle East for the next two years in a variety of roles and was equipped with Bristol Fighter aeroplanes which were used in cooperation with army duties. No. 208 Squadron was then moved to Greece in September 1922 to help the Greeks stem the Turkish advance on Constantinople, known as the Chanak Crisis. However, MacLaren was required to remain in the Middle East, as that was where his influence, knowledge and understanding lay.

At that time Somaliland—also known as 'The Horn of Africa'—was a British protectorate and was useful because it supplied the nearby British Indian outpost of Aden with food and other provisions. Aden was essential for Britain because it was on the 'short route' to India, meaning trade with the coastal tribes was important.[4] But there was a great deal of turmoil going on, as the British were not considered in favour and the 'Mad Mullah'—the religious and patriotic leader of the Somali people—had been fighting against British colonial rule for some time. So, in order to keep some control in Somaliland, Air Marshal Sir Hugh Trenchard considered that the RAF should be sent in to assume responsibility and support the army in controlling any local unrest.

MacLaren now became involved, and he was duly sent to Somaliland to be one of the squadron commanders to lead a detachment to Aden during this period. The Aden flight consisted of a two-seater open-cockpit de Havilland DH9 and a light bomber aircraft, which were sent in to lead the campaign to finally eradicate the Mad Mullah and bring Somaliland back under the British protectorate. This proved to be successful although it was not without loss of life. However, it was noted from the headquarters of the RAF in Cairo that the operations that were carried out had called for qualities of foresight, adaptability and determination, and their conspicuous success could not have been attained unless these qualities had been possessed to a marked degree by the officer in command and other personnel engaged in the operations.

In March 1922, in the honours list of awards to the RAF in Iraq, MacLaren was awarded the Distinguished Flying Cross (DFC) for his active service operations in Somaliland. Then on 30 June, he was promoted from flight lieutenant to squadron leader after notification was sent by the governor of the Somaliland Protectorate to Winston Churchill, secretary of state for the colonies, saying:

> I beg leave to request that the name of Flight Lieutenant MacLaren, Commanding Aden Flight, may be brought to the most favourable

notice of the Air Ministry for such recognition as they may think fit in connection with his valuable services here.[5]

On hearing of MacLaren's promotion to Squadron Leader, Trenchard was one of the first to congratulate him:

30th June, 1922

Dear MacLaren

Many congratulations on your promotion. From the way in which you have commanded the Flight at Aden, I am sure you will continue to do good work for the Royal Air Force in the higher rank to which you have now attained, and I shall follow your future career with very great interest.

Yours sincerely
H. Trenchard

Years later, MacLaren's daughter, Anna recounted a story she had been told by her father during his time in Aden. He had taken Ras Tafari Makonnen—who later became Emperor Haile Selassie of Ethiopia and was known well to MacLaren—for a quick flight in a biplane. Having never seen an airplane before, Ras Tafari was captivated by this demonstration of their power and abilities. He also insisted on taking his red umbrella with him, as he would not be parted from it!

As a result of this experience, he afterwards advocated the development of the Imperial Ethiopian Air Force.

MacLaren was to receive a letter of thanks from Ras Tafari's personal assistant:

Aden 4th November 1922

Dear MacLaren

The Air Force were splendid yesterday, and other days before kept the Ras in ecstasy from beginning to end of his visit. He was exclaiming like a little boy at the nose diving and other stunts and he asked me just before I left to convey to you and your officers his most sincere thanks for all you had done for him. He waived aside all formality and ran to the side of the ship to watch the final stunts, after he had embarked. I am sure his memories of Aden will be centred on his air flight and the other wonders in the air which he saw.

If we manage to push up a better show than our friends over the water, it will be largely due to you.

I would like to thank you personally and your officers for your great efforts to make Ras Tafari's visit a success.

The photographs arrived and are very much appreciated.

Yours sincerely

Sir Hugh Trenchard, writing to MacLaren from the Air Ministry in London in April 1922, commended him in many ways:

My dear MacLaren

I am very much interested in your reports of your flight to Somaliland and the wonderful work you have done. I hope you will receive the appreciation of the Air Council in due course.

It is with the very greatest interest that I read what you do, and what I like is that you always do more than I say you can do. This shows that it is you people who are building up the reputation of the Air Force as I always maintain, and I sincerely hope you will continue to carry on in the way you have done in the past. It is wonderful to find that so many of your machines are serviceable, and that you have had so few crashes.

The best of luck to you all in the future.

9

Proposal for the World Flight

With all MacLaren's experience of the Aden flight and of piloting some of the longest flights from England to Egypt and India, together with his wonderful sense of adventure, he decided to attempt to make the first flight around the world. He was now 30 years old.

On 29 June 1922, while still in Aden, he wrote to Sir Hugh Trenchard with the beginnings of his idea:

Dear Sir Hugh Trenchard

I should very much like to take this opportunity of making a request, which has been in my mind for some time.

I wrote to Messrs Vickers Ltd and Messrs Napier some few weeks ago, asking them if they would allow me to carry on the prepared flight round the world, which was to have been attempted by the late Ross-Smith, and submitted to them, that, if they concurred, I would send in an officiation to the Air Ministry for special permission.

I am, however, very doubtful if Messrs Vickers Ltd will concur, but think that Messrs Napier might, as they promised me some time ago, that, in the event of my undertaking another long flight, they would again discuss the question of supplying engines. Would it, therefore, be possible, in the event of Messrs Vickers Ltd refusing, for the Air Ministry to make me the loan of a suitable machine for this flight, provided permission is granted for me to attempt it. I would undertake to make all financial arrangements myself, and naturally, as a serving member of the RAF would accept any prizes, decorations etc which might become due to me, if I were to successfully complete the flight.

My chief ambition in life is to be the first to fly round the world, not so much for myself, but for the sake of the Service and British prestige. I would propose to start somewhere about the middle of next April.

In 1915, Vickers Ltd (Aviation Department) were manufacturing aeroplanes at Brooklands in Surrey and had developed a series of pusher biplanes which MacLaren considered were the right sort of aircraft for his venture. Vickers were one of England's longest established engineering companies and had a leading role in the development of aviation for almost seventy years.

In Aden, MacLaren met Flying Officer William Noble Plenderleith, who, after two years with 56 Squadron at Aboukir, Egypt, had then served with the Aden flight for a year. MacLaren considered that he was 'an excellent lad and a first-class pilot, and I hope that he will be able to accompany me in my attempt to fly round the world, if sanction is accorded. My proposed crew are myself, Plenderleith, and a first class N.C.O. fitter. I should like to make it an all RAF show.'

Plenderleith was born in Rosewell, Midlothian and joined the RAF as a cadet in 1917. He was not long gaining his wings and commission and was badly wounded as a fighter pilot in France with 54 Squadron in April 1918. He was later involved in the defence of London and gained valuable experience in night flying as well as being posted to the Marine Aircraft Experimental Establishment (MAEE) in Felixstowe, Suffolk, where he also gained experience on seaplanes and amphibious aircraft.[1]

However, any decisions from the Air Ministry were delayed until 8 August due to the political unrest in Constantinople, which had blocked passage to the Middle East. It was then that Trenchard replied:

My dear MacLaren.
With regard to your letter of June 29th, in which you ask to be allowed to fly round the world, we would have done a good deal

to have helped you if it had not been that Major Blake had started and got a good way on his way; and I think, therefore it would be advisable to wait before giving sanction and arranging conditions. We should have to put you on half-pay, I am afraid, for the time being if we eventually agreed; but now Blake is on his way write and let me know whether you feel that that fact interferes with your plans, and what are the financial arrangements you would make. I suppose this means that you would want to be able to lecture and publish a book, and various things of that sort, and that all you would want from us is the loan of a machine and some spares and to put you on half pay. Let me know how long you would want to be on half-pay, etc. You must not assume from this letter that we shall sanction the flight for certain, but anyhow I am quite keen to hear about it from you.

Yours sincerely
H Trenchard

Major W. T. Blake and Captain Norman Macmillan (his pilot) had set off on 24 May 1922 on their attempt to be the first to fly round the world. They departed from Croydon on a de Havilland DH-9 biplane and then took over a Fairey F-3 Floatplane when they reached Calcutta in India. This was a more suitable machine as they had to fly over large expanses of water. They had an extremely difficult journey with many forced landings and finally had to give up on the flight when they sank in the Bay of Bengal on 25 August.

Trenchard's reply to MacLaren was sent before Blake's flight had ended, so there was still no understanding as to whether another around-the-world flight attempt might be considered. But because of the sad failure of Blake's attempt, a further letter to MacLaren from Sir Hugh Trenchard on 28 December still considered that there was no immediate prospect of him obtaining sanction for a flight round the world. His immediate points were:

A world flight in which the Air Ministry is in any way involved must succeed, or a tremendous loss of prestige will result... the recent attempt of Blake did immense harm to the cause of aviation in India and the East, and we cannot risk another failure.

The Air Ministry considered that the flight should be carried out by private enterprise as there would then be money to be made out of it by advertisement, cinema rights, lectures and possibly a book. They also felt that MacLaren's timetable and understanding of how the flight would evolve was too optimistic.

It was finally agreed that MacLaren be given leave with half pay for the duration of the flight and an allowance to make the necessary arrangements with civil firms.

A further letter was then written by MacLaren to Trenchard outlining a schedule of times and landing grounds for the journey as well as the type of machine he decided would be the best:

> I am very much in favour of using the Vickers Viking Amphibian with Napier Lion Engine, as I consider the use of an amphibian essential. I have had a certain amount of correspondence with both Messrs Vickers and Messrs Napier and I think the former will do a great deal for me... the combination of the Air Ministry, Messrs Vickers and Messrs Napier should contribute very materially towards the success of the flight.

MacLaren returned to England from Aden and from June 1923 was sent to No. 1 School of Technical Training RAF in Buckinghamshire, home of the Aircraft Apprentice Scheme, where men were being trained in the mechanical trades for aircraft maintenance. It was there that he met Sergeant William Herbert Andrews, who had joined the RFC in September 1915. Andrews was later posted to 43 Squadron in France and then to 206 Squadron at Kantara, Egypt. He had been promoted to sergeant instructor, engines, and MacLaren invited him to join the crew as flight engineer/ fitter/rigger for the flight, which he duly accepted.[2]

There was one other crew member who would join them later in the flight as a navigator for the venture's Pacific stages. Lieutenant Colonel Louis Edgerton Broome, a logistics expert, had served with the Royal Engineers in the First World War and had previously worked as an engineer on the Panama Canal project. He had already been involved in the unsuccessful Blake/MacMillan flight. With the aid of the Canadian naval trawler HMCS *Thiepval*, he would establish supply bases and lay catchments of rations, fuel and equipment along the chain of uninhabited islands and tiny settlements from Japan, via the Aleutians, to North Alaska for that part of their journey.

During all this organisation and planning, MacLaren's wife Amanda gave birth to their third child in Paddington, London. Archibald Hugh (known as Hugh) was born on 2 November 1923, but it would seem that his father did not have much time to get to know him very well.

On 1 December, MacLaren was moved to the MAEE in Felixstowe. This was a former RNAS seaplane base where they designed, tested and evaluated seaplanes and flying boats. Plenderleith was also posted there and was to gain experience of piloting seaplanes and amphibious aircraft.

This, along with the rest of MacLaren's professional experience, not to mention his enthusiastic desire and wonderful sense of adventure, would stand him in good stead in his attempt to fly round the world.

10

Start of the World Flight— Southampton to Cairo

Time was now progressing and there was a great deal to organise to get everything ready for the world flight scheduled to start in March 1924.

Vickers had agreed to sponsor the flight and provide MacLaren with two amphibious biplanes. The expense was justified in terms of the experience likely to be gained in the endeavour. These planes were to be variants of the original Vickers Viking aircraft, all of which were designed by Rex Pierson and built by Vickers Ltd in Weybridge. They were to be named Vickers Vultures.

The two Vulture aircraft, both of which were registered as commercial four-seater flying boats had the registrations G-EBHO and G-EBGO. They were the only two ever built as a private venture for the round-the-world flight, and some necessary modifications were made to assist the crew with weather and landing variations across the world.

The hull was a conventional wooden flying-boat construction covered in mahogany ply, and the flying surfaces were fabric-covered. In order to be able to alight on water or land, the undercarriage, which lay against the side of the fuselage, could be cranked up and down by hand from the cockpit. Each plane had a four-bladed 'pusher' propeller, and a spare propeller in two halves was to be carried within the rear fuselage. Dual controls were fitted as well as an auxiliary oil tank and a drinking water tank that could be lifted out and used for cooling purposes if necessary.

Navigation would be achieved with a compass provided by H. Hughes and Son, maps designed by Stanfords map makers, an aneroid barometer, engine revolution counter and a Reid and Sigrist turn-and-bank indicator. Behind the navigator's position was fitted a very neat little chest of drawers to house all these charts and navigational aids. There was no wireless. An Aldis lamp was fitted on the nose for night landing as well as a 25lb anchor with cable.

The aero engine designer D. Napier and Son provided four 450hp 12-cylinder Lion engines especially for the flight, three low compression engines plus one high compression engine, which was to be sent to Montreal for fitting prior to the Atlantic crossing. The low compression engine meant that the Vulture could be run on the lower grades of aircraft fuel more commonly used by some of the countries along their route. Shell Mex supplied the gasoline. With 317 gallons of fuel on board and a cruising speed of approximately 85 mph, it was considered that they could achieve around 1,600 miles between refuelling.

It was intended that photography was to have played an important part in the historical record of the expedition and over 15,000ft of film and more than 700 photographic plates were distributed along the route in readiness for their arrival. Under the floor of the front cockpit was an ingenious nest of felt-lined boxes housing cinematograph and aerial cameras, films and plates, although there is very little evidence that these were actually used by the crew, so it is possible that they were left behind at the start to reduce weight.

The pilot and navigator (Plenderleith and MacLaren) were to be seated in the back cockpit, with the flight engineer (Andrews) sitting in front of them.

The Times had the reporting rights and Burberry provided them with coats. Weight was very important on the plane and each of the crew's luggage could not exceed 10 lbs. They were allowed a small weekend case in which to carry the things required. They all wore civilian clothes and were allowed one extra suit and one change of underclothes.[1] They also stored a sporting gun, a fishing rod with extra hooks, iron rations and tinned beef because, apparently, they planned to have lunch in the air and dine on land.[2]

Sergeant Andrews spent some time firstly at Napier Works in Acton to learn about the engine, and then at Vickers to get to know the Vulture aircraft and to learn everything about the plane. He also helped to build the second plane (G-EBGO) and pack it into crates to be shipped to Tokyo in case it was needed.

MacLaren and Plenderleith visited Vickers several times while he was there, and they all did several local test flights. MacLaren then spent months collecting information on landmarks, weather conditions, navigational bearings, compass variation, local time changes and any special difficulties or obstacles about aerodromes and water landings—everything necessary to make sure of the success of their venture. The three crew then met up in London, where they did a tour of the embassies to get all the visas needed for the countries they would visit during the flight.

The route was planned from west to east, starting from Calshot on Southampton Water, heading down through France, Italy and the Mediterranean to Cairo, on through India, Burma and China, then up through Japan, Kamchatka (Russia) and the Aleutian Islands to Alaska. They would then continue across Canada to Newfoundland, crossing the Atlantic via the Azores to Portugal, Spain and back through France, via Paris, to London. The total distance planned was 23,254 miles with an estimated flying time of 293 hours.

RAF bases giving logistical assistance were promised as far as Calcutta, India, but after that the crew were very much on their own and would have to rely on their own resources. The plan was to cross the Bay of Bengal and stop at Rangoon and Bangkok, before turning north-east, away from the equator, across Siam, Indochina, Hong Kong and Shanghai, before starting the 500-mile flight across the East China sea to the most southerly point of Japan. In Tokyo, a ten-day stopover was planned for an engine replacement and craft overhaul in readiness for the punishing journey to Vancouver. This part of the flight was over land and sea via the Kuril Islands, Kamchatka and the Aleutian Islands to Alaska, and around the coast to Vancouver. A large part of this section was desolate and fog-infested with many of the islands mainly volcanic. There was also a great risk of the plane running into flocks of large, slow-moving birds which could well result in a broken propeller. All this had to be taken into account.

The Canadian Air Force and the Canadian Pacific Fleet would await them at Vancouver and give them considerable assistance on their way across Canada. A second engine replacement was planned at Montreal, where seven days had been scheduled for the fitting of a higher compression unit to allow the Atlantic crossing to be made. This was necessary to provide a greater power output for the same fuel consumption, which together with the provision of an additional 77 gallon fuel tank would provide the necessary increased flying range for the crossing. Also, for the first time, the Vulture was to be fitted with a wireless, so that emergency contact with shipping could be used if necessary.

However, at the same time that MacLaren announced his plans, there was an announcement from the US government of an attempt to fly round the world in the opposite direction by four US Army aeroplanes, leaving Los Angeles on 15 March 1924. It later transpired that Italy, Portugal, Argentina and France were also planning an attempt but any likelihood of success rested mostly with the British or American airmen.

On 24 March, Plenderleith and Andrews, with the Vickers test pilot, Captain Cockerell, took off on G-EBHO from the Vickers factory at Weybridge to begin the round-the-world journey from Calshot Spit on Southampton Water. At the time, Calshot Naval Air Station was a testing ground for operating aircraft from water and the home of the Sunderland Flying Boat. On arrival at Calshot they were winched up a slipway and spent a busy time preparing for their final departure on the following morning.

And so it was that on Monday 25 March 1924, the journey began. The day dawned fine but misty, and many spectators and dignitaries arrived to see them off, including Air Ministry officials, personal friends and other visitors to wish them good fortune with a rousing chorus of 'Beat the Yanks!'

MacLaren's wife, Amanda, was there with their son Wallace (aged 6) and daughter Anna (aged 4) to make sure they got off safely.

Squadron Leader Cunningham Morris reported:

It was sentiment and strained emotion, the clinging lips of wife and children in an impressive, yet pathetic farewell, rather than a blare of trumpets and the plaudits of an enthusiastic crowd, that characterised the send-off of Squadron Leader A Stuart-MacLaren at Calshot, on March 25th, on his great round-the-world flight; and while there were numerous officials and service friends of the aviator present to witness the start and give the intrepid birdman a rousing cheer as they took to the air, yet it was the modest little family group, a few heart to heart words whispered, the purport of which none outside that group will ever know, a tender kiss, a hug, and a cheery "take care of yourselves, I'll be back soon" that marked the moments prior to the departure, and gave an insight into the nature of the man, that with little concern, except for leaving his loved ones behind, was starting on his "great adventure" that might prove an historic feat and bring fresh laurels to British aviation and no small fame to the leader and his colleagues.

To those who know the calibre of this man, MacLaren, and his big heartedness, there was far more pride and thrill to him in the final caress of his bonny wife and children, the parting embrace, the farewell wave, than in any ostentatious display of ceremony or the acclamations of an admiring populace on the occasion of his "send-off". And yet perhaps no man was more appreciative of the enthusiasm of his friends and officials of MacLaren, modestly accepting as always more on behalf of his profession as an aviator and the prestige of British aviation, than for himself or his own personal ability and aggrandizement.

MacLaren loves flying for flying's sake, devoting his whole being to his work while in the air, and looking at the science of aviation more as an inspiration than a material accomplishment.[3]

Amanda went on a warm-up flight down Southampton water with Plenderleith and the Vickers test pilot, Captain Cockerell. She said that she regretted that she could not come on the trip: 'It is a splendid machine and my husband is delighted with it.'[4]

The bronze metal mascot, Marmaduke, was then fitted onto the front of the fuselage by Amanda, as it had been with MacLaren on each one of his successful flights to Egypt and India, to bring him good luck. Then a certain amount of newly minted gold sovereigns in a plain leather bag were stowed safely and securely away in case of need in many of the primitive regions they would be visiting.

MacLaren was heard to say: 'I am sanguine we shall succeed. We have a wonderful machine.'

As departure drew near, a telegram arrived for MacLaren from King George V:

BUCKINGHAM PALACE
The King desires me to convey to you, Flying Officer Plenderleith, and Sergeant Andrews, his best wishes for the success of the great enterprise on which you are embarking today. His Majesty will follow with deep interest the progress of your flight.
Private Secretary

The secretary of state of air, Lord Thompson, who had come down especially to witness the departure of the three serving members of the RAF, made the following short speech:

I feel certain that I am expressing all your thoughts when I say to Squadron Leader MacLaren, Flying Officer Plenderleith, and Sergeant Andrews, how proud we are of them and their high courage. Our hearts and hopes will go with them through the innumerable vicissitudes of this world flight. We know that only superhuman obstacles will prevent them succeeding in their effort. We trust that their energy and skill will triumph in the end. We bid them God-speed and we will promise them a splendid welcome on their safe return.[5]

Many other dignitaries were also present to witness the start of the flight including Air Vice Marshall Sir Geoffrey Salmond, Mr Muller (Superintendent at Vickers Aircraft Works at Weybridge), Mr Rex Pierson (designer of the machine) and Mr Vane, managing director of D. Napier and Son Ltd.

The Vulture set off at 1200 and taxied out into the water for takeoff. With an escort to the Isle of Wight of two F.5 Flying Boats and three Avro Bison planes, they headed out down the Solent on the first stage of the flight.

However, MacLaren's log showed that within 35 minutes they ran into bad weather and fog off the coast of France:

Left Calshot at 1206; Ryde 1215. Steamer going East; skirted coast to avoid rain storms. Passed Bembridge Point 1219; air singularly free of bumps; weather appears to be brightening.

1242. Ran into low cloud and mist, 600ft; visibility 500 yards; sea very calm.

1250. Dropped to 400ft; clouds appear to follow us down; can barely see the sea. Dropping to 300ft; fog and mist getting thicker.

1305. Only at 100ft; visibility less than 50 yards.

1310. Cannot see anything; altimeter shows 50ft.

1315. Altered course to strike coast sideways—as estimate should reach at 1320—rising to 100ft. Visibility nil; all eyes watching

1325. Cliffs suddenly at 50 yards ahead. Plenderleith, with magnificent presence of mind, opened full throttle and made Immelmann turn with bank of 90 degrees, missing cliffs by only a few feet.

1328. Landed in sea, all as white as sheets. Reckon position just SW Etretat; taxying along coast 50 yards from shore, just visible towards Le Havre.

Arrived outskirts Le Havre 1450; moored to buoy 1505; weather here like pea soup.

Hope to push on to Lyon tomorrow morning. Machine and engine splendid throughout.

On going ashore at Le Havre, MacLaren and Plenderleith visited the British consul to make arrangements for an overnight stay at the Frascati Hotel, while Andrews was left in charge of the Vulture on its mooring for the night, with a motorboat standing by to assist in case a wind change should cause him any trouble.

Unfortunately, there was no improvement in the weather, and on Wednesday 26 March they took off at 1053 towards Lyon from rough seas in rain and squall, flying at an altitude of 1,700ft and experiencing many heavy rain showers. As they passed Rouen at 1125 they ran into very bumpy air, and the undercarriage was lowered in case a quick descent should become necessary. They then caught a glimpse of the Eiffel Tower as they passed Paris.

The weather continued to be full of rainstorms, although there were patches of clearer skies. They finally arrived at Bron Aerodrome, Lyon at 1545, having completed 325 miles in four hours forty minutes. They were welcomed by the director of the Bron Civil Air Station, a number of French army officers and several English residents of Lyon as they came to rest in front of a line of hangers in the centre of the airfield.

MacLaren's log read: 'We had a fine trip, especially after we got into the Saone Valley and left the rain behind—but we are all starving.' They were also suffering from deafness, having neglected to use ear protectors during the flight. The aircraft was refuelled, housed in one of the hangars and given a routine service check for the takeoff to Rome the following day.

On Thursday 27 March, the Vulture took off at 1100 hours. But with yet more adverse weather conditions, they decided to change course and reached Civitavecchia, north-west of Rome, at 1800, feeling very tired from the long detour and bad weather. Once again, they landed in the harbour and stayed overnight in order to rest before continuing the remaining miles to Rome Airport.

The next day, on 28 March, an early start was made to Centocelle Airport in Rome, but in taking off from the harbour they unfortunately hit a piece of driftwood which smashed the port side float. However, as there was no other damage, they continued on and safely landed at 0750. Here they decided to stop over for a couple of days for repairs to the port side float.

Newspapers reported that many visitors came to see the aircraft while they were there, including General Piccio, who was commanding the Italian air force, Signor Finzi, the vice commissioner of aviation, and the British and American ambassadors. The latter inadvertently put his foot in a can of engine oil upsetting it all over the cockpit and ruining his clothes. He was later heard to remark that it had all been well worth it, just to have been able to see over the British aircraft!

Their stopover was then extended for repairs to a tank which had been slightly damaged and a general check of the aircraft.

At 0625 on Monday 31 March, they set off once again for Brindisi, in Southern Italy on the coast of the Adriatic Sea, hoping to arrive in Athens on the same day. The farewell ceremony was witnessed by Signor Mercanti, the intendant general and a number of senior Italian air force officers. Before they left, MacLaren expressed his warmest appreciation for all the assistance, kindness and hospitality shown to him and his crew during their stay.

MacLaren's log shows that once again the weather was appalling:

We were groping about in near pitch darkness. Then a small gap appeared in the clouds—flying at 100ft we found ourselves in a small valley and to our joy saw a railway line. This gave me a clue to our position, but I don't know what we should have done if we had come to a tunnel—we should either have gone through leaving our wings behind, or gone aloft to don other and better ones.

His log also commends Plenderleith's great skill in preserving direction so accurately in the face of such adverse conditions.

They finally arrived at the naval aerodrome in Brindisi at 1045 to await weather clearance but had great difficulty bringing the Vulture in under a strong crosswind. Many men plunged into the water and managed to get a line to the machine, but when they tried to haul her in, the load was too much and it broke. A second attempt was met with greater success, and Plenderleith brought them out of the water.

By 1230 the weather had cleared nicely, and they set off again at 1243 towards Athens, where a large gathering of local people, British patriots, reporters and cameramen were waiting. But at midnight the Athens wireless station received a message from them that the flight was to be delayed. However, nothing more was heard of the Vulture until after 1530 the following day.

According to MacLaren's log the reason was a terrific vibration in the engine, causing them to shut it off and bring the plane down. Plenderleith had fortunately managed to make an excellent landing on Lake Korissia, a lagoon at the southernmost end of the island of Corfu, and as the strong winds were blowing them, they steadily drifted inshore. The machine was grounded about 100 yards out in 2 ft of water, and MacLaren waded ashore.

The Times was to report:

> Squadron Leader MacLaren set out to find some sort of communication
> with the town. After trudging about ten miles he came to the village
> of Aghios Mathias, from which, with some difficulty, he telephoned
> to the British Consul. Then he returned to his machine on horseback
> with provisions. He declares that the inhabitants of the village were
> very kind on hearing they were British, and offered all possible
> assistance. The only food available was black bread, cheese, eggs
> and good local wine, for which the airman paid with Greek money
> borrowed from a native. MacLaren and Plenderleith are each
> collecting a set of stamps from each place they land. They stick them
> in an album with the date stamp of the local post office. This will
> form a very interesting record.[6]

A preliminary examination of the engine indicated that the reduction
gear (the gears between the engine drive shaft and the propeller) had
completely stripped, a replacement for which would need to be sent
out from England. They hoped this would only take a few days. That
night they slept in the machine and the following morning MacLaren
and Plenderleith walked into the main city—also called Corfu—
leaving Andrews to start work on the engine.

As luck would have it, they managed to get a lift in a car and were
returned later on with a small tent and sufficient provisions for the
next few days. Unfortunately, though, Andrews had discovered that
there was more serious damage in the form of a cracked crankcase,
and it was possible that a completely new engine would be needed.
MacLaren managed to contact Napier by numerous telegrams,
and after hours of waiting for replies, it was decided that a new
engine was to be sent overland to Brindisi, together with a new
spare float from Vickers. Also a skilled Napier engineer had already
been despatched to them with every conceivable part which could
be wanted in connection with the reduction gear. He was reported
to have flown from Croydon to Paris on the evening of 2 April,
continuing by rail to Brindisi, and hopefully arriving in time to catch
the Thursday boat for Corfu. Luckily, many stops were being pulled
out by a lot of people.

Three weeks passed waiting for the new engine to arrive, before they could continue the journey to Athens. In the meantime they stayed in the small tent they had been given and relied on periodic deliveries of food from Corfu. Fortunately, the weather was sunny and calm, which helped the crew to relax after the terrible weather thus far experienced.

As the machine was still lying on the beach between Lake Korissia and the sea, and they decided to get it into the sea and tow it to Corfu Harbour. Fortunately, a British warship, HMS *Wishart*, happened to be in the harbour at the time. Her crew lent a hand to haul the Vulture across a spit of land separating the lake from the sea, then the warship towed her back along the coast to Corfu.

MacLaren later wrote an article for *The Times* on 16 April:

On Monday the 14th at 1 o'clock in the afternoon a Lloyd Tristino ship arrived with the new engine and float, a Cook's courier, and a mechanic from Napier's. I went on board and persuaded the master that Customs examination was unnecessary, as the engine was being taken on board the *Emperor of India*. We lowered the engine and the float and proceeded to the *Emperor of India*, where they were hoisted on board. The machine was towed across to the *Emperor of India* by a whaler and moored alongside. A wind from the North made the sea too choppy to risk putting in the new engine. The *Emperor of India*, therefore, was turned slightly to give her lee. The old engine was hoisted on board and crated, and the machine was towed round and moored astern. Preparations were then made to beach the machine early next morning. We went to bed feeling a lot more cheerful. On Tuesday morning we beached the machine and spent the whole day installing the new engine. With the aid of two naval mechanics and our own, we got her completed by 1730. We then ran the engine up and found it OK, giving full revolutions. Then we put the cowling on, got all our stuff on board, launched her, and gave her half an hour's trial flight. Everything was OK. The machine was none the worse for the little experience on Lake Korissia. We moored astern of the *Emperor of India*, and got everything ready for departure this (Wednesday) morning. If it had not been for the British Fleet we should probably have been there another fortnight as no facilities whatsoever exist, either at Lake Korrissia or Corfu, for installing an engine, and we should have had to take the engine to pieces and rebuild it in situ.

This morning, Wednesday, we got everything on board, taxied round the harbour for ten minutes to warm up the engine, and then rose from the water just opposite the *Emperor of India*. We could hear the cheers of the crew above the noise of the engine. We circled round the harbour once and then headed south.

Two days later they were once more heading south to Athens. The *Vulture* had an excellent flight from Corfu, taking three hours and twenty minutes, circling over the Acropolis and finally landing on the sea by Phaleron Naval Aerodrome, the naval seaplane station at Athens. They were met by a Greek naval cutter's crew who did the honours by taking them in tow as far as the slipway. Then Plenderleith taxied up the slipway and along to the aerodrome. An official reception party watched and Captain Hadjikyriakos, the Greek Minister of Marine with a group of Naval Officers gave great cheers of '*Zito!*' [Hurrah], followed by resounding three cheers from the British spectators.

The crew and other special guests were then invited to the Greek officers' mess for refreshments, where MacLaren said that the *Vulture* was now in fine fettle with its new engine and that the flight from Corfu had been their best so far because of the better weather. He once again took the chance to express warm appreciation of the help given them by the officers and men on the British warships at Corfu.

The following day, on 17 April at 0800, they taxied out for takeoff for the next stage of the journey across the Mediterranean and then along the desert airmail route from Cairo to Baghdad. Increasing their speed for lift off, they were to continue on the water surface until almost out of sight. However, because of the very calm water, this was proving impossible and they had to return to the airdrome at Phaleron. They then made the decision to offload 25 gallons of petrol in order to lighten their load, and once again setting off, they rose from the water and began to fly southwards.

MacLaren logged their progress in minute detail each step of the way:

11.38	Left Greek coast behind; estimated speed 83.5mph. Weather beautifully calm.
12.11	Passed Seripho Isle, climbed to 2,000 ft.
12.46	Passed Polykandro Isle, speed 84mph.
14.08	Cape Sidero. Altered course for Alexandria.
14.30	Lunched on board.
16.00	Passed two small birds flying North; half way across Mediterranean.
16.25	Over Steamship Waverley going due East.
17.45	Sighted land.
18.15	Passed Aboukir; dropped message in biscuit tin asking them to wireless Heliopolis.
18.39	Passed Damanhur. Dusk coming on; moon nearly full.
19.20	Sighted Heliopolis lights.
19.40	Landed O.K., with aid of flares.

The 'biscuit tin' message had been dropped into the sea and was fortunately retrieved by the authorities at Aboukir. The officer commanding 216 Squadron at RAF Heliopolis was thus informed of their intended arrival and ensured that the landing ground was prepared and flares made ready for their arrival.

The Vulture arrived at 1930 and Plenderleith made a beautiful landing beside the flares. The ground staff ran in to take hold of the wingtips, and the machine taxied to a nearby hanger, where it was to be housed for the night.

The Times reported:

Squadron Leader MacLaren's entry into Cairo this evening was heralded by a whirring noise from the north. Thousands of eyes scanned the deep blue vault of the Egyptian sky, but with the Easter moon shining brilliantly Squadron Leader MacLaren was not showing any visible lights, only this mysterious whirr from the blue denoting his course across the city of Heliopolis. He had a splendid flight in ideal weather conditions.[7]

The flight from Athens to Cairo was one of the longest flying times throughout the whole journey—eight hours and forty-five minutes in fine weather conditions.

This was the first RAF port of call on the flight, and MacLaren and his crew were greeted as guests of 216 Squadron by the commanding officer and taken to the Squadron Mess where they enjoyed a welcome whisky and soda. The crew were reported to have been remarkably fresh after their long flight of eight hours and forty-five minutes, although once again they were suffering from a slight deafness due to continuous engine noise. MacLaren was, of course, no stranger to 216 Squadron having been their flight commander in 1920 before moving to Aden.

The next day was spent preparing for an early start the following morning for the second part of the journey.

With the attempt to achieve the flight round the world by the Americans, British and others now underway, Lucien Blin Desbled, a lecturer in aeronautics, put forward his views about the impact of aviation on the future in an article entitled 'Flying Around the World? What are its Uses?', published in *The Sunday Times* on 20 April 1924. The world had become familiar with airplanes as machines for war in defense and attack, and the possibilities for other purposes had yet to emerge.

A COMING REVOLUTION

After flying some 1,500 miles each, both the American and British airmen, who, for different reasons, had been forced to delay their flight round the world, have now resumed their journey. These two attempts to circle the globe by air began, it will be remembered, towards the end of March, and within a few days of each other. The British airmen set out from Southampton towards the rising sun, and the Americans in a westerly direction from Seattle. Apart from the portion across the Atlantic Ocean, the two courses, planned independently, lie fairly close to each other. In both cases the crossing of the Atlantic will constitute the big last lap home. The British airmen propose to effect it from St. John's via the Azores, to Lisbon, whilst the chosen American Atlantic route lies much further north by way of Iceland and Greenland.

In spite of the mishaps and delays which both expeditions have met in the early stages of their flight, they are both determined to do their best to complete their journey round the globe.

There are many, even in the aeronautical world, who have not yet understood the possibilities opened up by the survival of such flights. To those who do not see beyond the immediate technical or commercial results these flights, even if they were crowned with complete success, seem futile and incapable of practical applications; and, to them, the risks incurred by the airmen, and the cost and anxiety thrust upon the organisers and sponsors of the undertakings, appear to be out of proportion to whatever profit may be derived from their realisation. But, in order to have right conception of what flying round the world may mean, it is necessary to bear in mind a few facts taken from the history of sea navigation after it was discovered that the world was round.

THE ADVENTURER SPIRIT

Bring back to your recollection the attempts made, and the hazards undergone, by those English, Dutch, French, and Portuguese adventurers—this word being used in its natural and undebased meaning—who, in the past, sailed out in their relatively frail craft and scoured the seas looking for fresh lands or for new routes to old lands. And, no doubt it is under the impulse of the same spirit, and moved by similar motives, that the British and American airmen have launched themselves into the uncharted air ocean.

It is to the sea adventurers of the past that we owe the discovery of such great sea routes as those round the Cape to the East and through the Straits of Magellan to the Pacific shores. That the utilisation of these routes, has for generations, influenced the history of the world, everybody is aware. It is also well-known that, unchallenged for a long time, the supremacy of these world routes was, in recent years, seriously discounted by the opening of the Suez Canal and of the Panama Canal. It is unnecessary to dwell upon the significance, both political and economic, which, by providing shorter world routes, the engineering feats of cutting canals across the isthmuses of Suez and Panama have had on the world, as we know it to-day. It is, however, well for us to remember a general lesson. This lesson is that the world is affected politically, economically, commercially, and in many other aspects, by the establishment of shorter and quicker means of world communication.

EAST AND WEST

We are accustomed to-day to think of travel to China or Japan in terms of East and West. If we look, however, at a geographical globe, we shall find that, in point of actual distance, these places are much nearer to us when the distances are measured, in north and south directions, through the Arctic regions. In truth it was this fact which induced many efforts—such as those of Hudson, Frobisher, Sir John Franklin—to open up the northern route. But if the ice proved an obstacle to those sea navigators of the past, just as it does to the modern ones, it cannot offer an impassable barrier to air navigation. Besides being the smallest of all the oceans, the Arctic is dotted with a large number of small islands, which will no doubt, assume unwonted value and considerable importance as soon as a regular air route is established through that region. But the discovery of a passage to the East, through the Arctic regions, is by no means the only way in which flying round the globe is capable of influencing the history of the world in the near future.

THE WORLD IS SHRINKING

When we look at a world's atlas and think of the route, extending over 24,000 miles, which the British airmen propose to follow, we have a distinct feeling that, metaphorically speaking, the world is shrinking before the aeroplane. Mountain chains, barren deserts, and oceans and continents offer no unsurpassable barrier to the air navigator. At an average speed of eighty miles per hour, the British airmen could, in theory, complete their journey in 300 flying hours. On the supposition that they could fly their machines all the time, it would take them less than thirteen days to describe their circle round the earth.

A study, even superficial, of the proposed route would constitute a useful geographical lesson. The selected route is from London, through Lyons, Rome, Brindisi, Athens, Cairo, Bagdad, and along the Persian Gulf, to India; then, after cutting right across India to

Calcutta, it would follow the coasts of Cochin-China and China to Tokyo; then, by way of the Kuril Islands, it would cut the eastern extremity of Siberia and cross the Pacific via the Aleutian Islands. Then, keeping close to the coast of Alaska, the airmen would reach Vancouver, whence they would fly across Canada and, finally, the Atlantic Ocean, calling at the Azores on their return to London via Portugal, Spain, and France.

ROOT OF A REVOLUTION

But more striking still than the speed of the new mode of world travel and the distance which the British airmen propose to travel, is the nature of the route selected by them. Being over land as well as over sea, it differs completely and fundamentally from the usual means of modern travel by rail or by sea. It is a free and bold combination of both.

And in this feature of air locomotion there lies the root of a revolution which, in the near future, must take place in the life and in travel on our globe. With the developments of air locomotion, which we may consider as assured, the attempts now being made to fly round the world are the heralds of those flights which, we may be certain, will, before long, displace the main currents of human activity. The world-changes for which railways and steam navigation are responsible will, in all probability, be small compared to the one which, in its very initial stage, is now being brought about by the round-the-world flight pioneers, and of which we are taking only a very casual notice. The establishment of world's air routes will have much greater political, economic, commercial, and social significance than even the cutting of the Isthmus of Suez and of that of Panama.[8]

11

Cairo to Karachi

By 0600 on Saturday 19 April, a considerable crowd of spectators had gathered at Heliopolis Aerodrome to witness MacLaren and Plenderleith arrive in a motor car from Cairo, where they had stayed overnight at the Shepheard's Hotel. The Vulture had been brought out of the hangar, and Andrews, who had had the hospitality of the sergeants' mess overnight, was busy making final touches for takeoff.

The engines were started at 0615 and the airmen climbed onboard. By 0646 they were making a clean rapid ascent. After climbing to 600 ft, they circled once round the aerodrome to wave farewell to the crowd. They then headed east in the direction of the Suez Canal, bound for El Ziza in Transjordan. This was on the edge of the Syrian desert and had been chosen for its situation on the Cairo-to-Baghdad airmail route, meaning it was marked and known to MacLaren.

However, within an hour after takeoff, there appeared to be a problem with the engine; it was decided to make a landing at Abu Sueir—about 60 miles north-east of Cairo and 8 miles west of Ismailia—to check it out. They made a safe landing at 0800 and ascertained a problem common to desert areas, namely the entry of very fine sand—constantly being borne on the wind and thermals— into the engine. They spent nearly two hours checking and cleaning the fuel supply system. MacLaren wrote in his log: 'Rotary pumps not functioning properly; landed to adjust them. Took off 10.02am.'

The biscuit tin message asking for help, which had been dropped into the sea before Aboukir, was also now handed back to them!

They followed the shores of the Dead Sea and then altered course towards Jerusalem, over which they passed at a height of 7,500 ft in very cold and bumpy weather. Making a slow descent into El Ziza, which lay on the very edge of the desert and was perfectly flat for miles around, they finally arrived at 1330. There was no real aerodrome there, just an RAF hut and petrol store with a station on the Hejaz railway line and a train once a fortnight.

Although the place was almost deserted, they found a small company of mechanics overhauling a machine, along with a detachment of armoured cars from Amman and a couple of private cars. According to *The Times*, the '[place] was deserted except for a few Bedouin who were totally puzzled by the strange aircraft with the body of a boat that had landed in their desert.'[1]

Later that afternoon Air Marshal Swann, the air officer commanding RAF Middle East, and Group Captain MacEwan, the officer commanding RAF Transjordan, who MacLaren had flown with to India in the Handley Page bomber *Old Carthusian* in May 1919, flew in from Amman, the capital of Jordan, to greet them.

Weather reports were now showing that a wind depression was moving in from the northern Arabian Peninsula with the risk of violent sandstorms, so MacLaren decided to make an early start for Baghdad as soon as possible. On 20 April they completed their pre-flight checks and were airborne at 0935 Egyptian time. They intended to continue following the airmail route across the Syrian desert to Baghdad, and they rose to 7,000 ft, where the wind was less strong but very cold.

The desert air mail was provided with a number of emergency landing grounds identified alphabetically by letter. They passed E at 1058, G at 1130, K at 1200, N at 1235 and R at 1313. They then lost sight of the track in difficult gravel country, having to take compass bearings to ascertain where they were. They finally passed landing ground V at 1430 and saw the Euphrates and Habbania rivers, then Baghdad in the distance. It was quite a relief after passing over the desert to see large areas of cornfields ripening for harvest.

They finally landed at Hinaidi RAF Aerodrome near Baghdad at 1620, stiff and frozen, but the engine was running very nicely and had performed well throughout the long flight of seven hours and

ten minutes. There were cheers from a large gathering of members of
RAF personnel, and they were welcomed by the high commissioner
and Lady Dobbs, the air vice-marshal, many officers and the American
consul.

At that time the clerical man in the Orderly Room in Hinaidi,
Joseph Edward Cape (known as Ted), also witnessed the aeroplane
landing and was heard to say:

> We had heard that a Squadron Leader MacLaren was due to arrive
> in a Vickers Amphibian, about April 20th on an attempt to fly around
> the World. A big crowd of us trooped out to the 'drome to see it land.
>
> It duly landed near one of the Squadrons, and Squadron Leader
> MacLaren got out most casually, dressed, as far as I can remember,
> in just a lounge suit and a trilby hat. He asked some of the airmen
> standing around to wheel the machine into the hanger, which we
> were proud to do.[2]

However, there was still a continuing threat of bad weather and
MacLaren was anxious to hasten on to Karachi to avoid the south-west
monsoon. The RAF station commander arranged to complete some
small necessary repairs for the Vulture overnight, as well as apply a
fresh coat of varnish to the hull of the machine.

A large crowd waved as they took off from Hinaidi at 0905 on
Monday 21 April and headed towards Basra and Bushire on the Persian
Gulf with an escort of three Bristol Fighters. It had been arranged the
night before that they would land at RAF Sheiba for lunch, and flying
at a height of 4000 ft with air conditions very bumpy, they could see a
large sandstorm building up fast and thick out on their port side. But
they were satisfied that it was unlikely to affect them.

As they approached RAF Sheiba they were met by two de Havilland
9A aircraft that had come out from RAF Sheiba to accompany them
to Basra and take over from the Bristol Fighters' escort. A few minutes
later the Bristol Fighters signalled their intended departure and with
a final wave from the leader broke away and headed back towards
Baghdad.

Finally landing at Sheiba Aerodrome at 1235, they had time to join
their hosts in the mess for drinks and lunch, but were a little delayed

due to a small repair to the hull, taking off again at 1533 in a strong north wind and turning south-east on course for Bushire. They then passed the Anglo-Persian oil reservoirs and found themselves heading into a sandstorm.

MacLaren's log was to read:

17.50	Encountered terrific bumps; discovered wind suddenly changed completely round, and now plumb against us.
18.30	Progress very slow; darkness fast coming on. Passed over fishing village Tezireh; decided to land, so fired Verey light to ascertain exact direction of wind.
18.35	Landed on sea.

They enlisted the help of the local fishermen, and using mainly sign language, they managed to anchor and secure the machine for the night. They had a hot uncomfortable night on the wing of the aircraft before leaving at first light for the short hop to Bushire, where breakfast and hot showers were eagerly awaited.[3]

Once they reached Bushire, MacLaren sent a telegram to *The Times*, detailing the progress of this stage of their journey:

Several native craft came out to meet us, which was fortunate, as we ran on a sand-bank while 'taxi-ing' shorewards. Andrews and I got out of the machine into a native boat in order to lighten the machine, and Plenderleith was able to get her off the soft sand undamaged, and she was towed up to the lee of the shore by three native sailing craft, and tied up astern of a fishing vessel, securely anchored. We slept fitfully on the plane, after a meal of sandwiches and oranges. Plenderleith nearly rolled off into the sea.

At the first sign of dawn we were up, and got the engine running. At 5.30 we took off from the water, and at 5.45 landed at Bushire Aerodrome safely. We are now filling up the machine with petrol oil and ourselves with food, and propose to leave for Bander Abbas this morning.[4]

At 1114 they took off once again for Bander Abbas, and with a favourable wind they were travelling at a speed of 87 mph. But they were then to encounter appalling bumpy weather and MacLaren reported: 'We were chucked about all over the place.'

However, the weather improved and half an hour later they were in sight of their destination and landed at 1546 on the sea opposite the British Consulate. They let down the wheels by hand and taxied through the surf and up onto the hard sand beach to a tremendous welcome by the local people, who were astonished to witness the aircraft lifting itself out of the water and coming ashore.

It was now 23 April and after spending a quiet night on the machine in front of the British Consulate, they took off from the beach at 0845 the following morning, with much waving and cheering from a delighted crowd. They arrived at the RAF aerodrome at Chah Bahr, Baluchistan at 1135. They refuelled and made all the checks, refreshed themselves and had some lunch before continuing on to Karachi at 1345.

It will be remembered that the only means of knowing their direction was by following their maps and compass directions, so their route to Karachi, written in MacLaren's log, read:

Simple route—no compass bearing, more like directions from a local tourist office—just turn left and follow the coast until it turns to the right,—and it's the next major city on the left.

This flight to Karachi was relatively easy, taking approximately four hours and fifteen minutes, and they arrived at the new Drigh Road RAF Aerodrome at 1800. MacLaren knew this aerodrome only too well, as he had already flown there in January 1918 in the Handley Page *Old Carthusian.*

There is no doubt that MacLaren and his crew were the most adventurous of men. A British newspaper article at the time reported:

MacLaren and those with him are not the kind of men to be affected by the inevitable risks of the stirring enterprise which they have undertaken. After making all their preparations with due care and forethought, they have set about it with a full realisation of the seriousness of the venture and yet in a light-hearted spirit, which will enable them to accept cheerfully anything which may turn up in the shape of what golfers would call rubs of the green, and make the best of them. The next stage of their journey, by Allahabad, Calcutta, Bangkok, and Hong Kong to Tokyo, is nearly 6000 miles in length. In the first part of this section they will be able to count, in case of need, on the continued support of their comrades of the Royal Air Force, in the same way as they have already benefited by the friendly help of the Royal Navy. The way that still lies before them is long and difficult. But, by what they have so far done in their British amphibian aircraft, they have shown that the mettle of which they are made is British all through.[5]

A further article in a British newspaper showed what an incredible accomplishment this flight was:

We read these stories nowadays with a certain lack of emotion, but the forethought and enterprise which go towards them ought to evoke both our sense of wonder and our feeling of respect. In a sense, such expeditions are putting such a challenge to machinery as has seldom been put before. Like the two pioneers who flew to Australia, they are asking the mechanisms which they employ to perform feats of endurance which would not be expected on the surface of the earth.

Steamships are different, because conditions of space and possibilities of weight carrying enable engines to be built in dimensions which make them as durable as the stationary powerplant in any factory. On the other hand, if one takes a train from Paris to Constantinople, or even from London to Aberdeen, one is aware that the engine is changed in the former case frequently, and in the second case at least twice or three times en-route. These changes may not be essential, but they have been considered desirable. Though, therefore, the attempt to fly from Southampton to Calcutta with the same engine would have provided, if it had been successful, an interesting and impressive spectacle of mechanical efficiency, it would really not have been much to the point in so far as the development of air travel over wide areas of the globe is concerned. In fact, the British airmen have got as far as India with one change of engine, which is much more than could be said of any train that has ever gone from the Channel coast to less than half the distance which they have traversed.[6]

The Vulture and its three crew had now completed the first stage of their epic journey, having flown some 5,000 miles since leaving England. The next stage from Karachi to Tokyo was estimated to be 6,000 miles. MacLaren had no previous experience of the route from here onwards, so they were to rely entirely on his preliminary planning.

12

Karachi to Calcutta

The Vulture and crew were very well received at Karachi and were warmly congratulated on their rapid passage from Baghdad. They were greeted by Mr Rieu, Commissioner in Sind, Major General H. F. Cooke, commanding the Sind Rajputana district, and other representative citizens. MacLaren took advantage of the assistance offered by the RAF authorities, under the command of Wing Commander W. C. Hicks, to examine the machine thoroughly and to tune it up before setting off the following day.

The new Napier engine, installed at Corfu, had worked perfectly up until now, and after some rest and much-needed proper sleep, they took off on Saturday 26 April after a Bristol Fighter had reconnoitred how far the low-lying mist obscured the route ahead. It came back with a favourable report, and they set off at 0709 in brilliant sunshine for Nasirabad in the Indian state of Rajasthan. However, they failed to arrive.

MacLaren's diary showed that they had passed Hyderabad, in the Sind province, an hour after leaving Karachi and then had entered the great Rajputana desert. Five minutes later, while flying at a height of 4,000 ft, the engine just stopped. Up to this moment the engine had been running perfectly, without a single misfire. The reduction gear had stripped again, and the crank case was broken. With the unpowered aircraft rapidly losing height, they all looked out for a suitable landing area. Plenderleith was to affect a perfect landing head up to the wind on a small path less encumbered by trees and small bushes, and without the slightest damage to the machine.

Very quickly they were surrounded by crowds of excited and curious people who seemed to appear from nowhere, but in fact had come from the nearby village of Kornra, which was in the Sind desert about two miles from Parlu railway station on the main Jodhpur–Bikaner Railway. The first thing the crew had seen were turbans moving among the trees; then hundreds of wondering Indians rushed up, clambered over the machine and touched the airmen. The Indians seemed frightened at first, but when reassured, were most helpful.

The headman of the village appeared on a pony and, using sign language, indicated that he would give every assistance. MacLaren borrowed another pony from the villagers and rode with the headman to Parlu station to wire ahead to Jodhpur and Karachi for assistance.

Plenderleith and Andrews remained with the machine and immediately set to work to protect the aircraft from the blazing sun with the help and assistance of a party of villagers. They all lifted the machine then put the nose under bushes and covered the body with wet cloths. The villagers then formed a guard to protect the machine.

At midnight the westbound mail train from Jodhpur arrived at Parlu; the authorities had kindly sent special refreshments and a sleeping car with food, cooks, servants and every comfort for the stranded airmen.

While all this wonderful assistance was taking place, MacLaren got the train from Parlu back to Karachi to try to arrange for a replacement engine, as it was clear that the damage was more serious than first thought. But an equivalent engine of the type required was unobtainable in India, and although a new engine could be supplied by Iraq Command, it would have to be brought to India by boat, and then overland from Karachi. Unfortunately, these engines were all high-compression ones of the 'tractor' type, for use with a front-fitted propeller. As the Vulture had a 'pusher' propeller at the back of the engine, it would need to be converted to accommodate it, and then changed again for a low-compression engine before they left India.

Andrews was already making preparations to remove the old engine in readiness for the arrival of the new one. Luckily the railway had plenty of spare wooden railway sleepers and lengths of steel rails, and it was suggested that these might be used to build a gantry to straddle the aircraft, from which they could fashion a simple pulley hoist. So, two square towers were built from sleepers, with lengths of rails to accommodate the pulley hoist. While all this was taking place, the crew decided to have some fun and so they went on a shooting trip, riding on camels.

In Iraq, the RAF were arranging for one of their Napier engines to be dispatched for use in the Vulture. It was to be shipped by fast boat from Basra on 3 May, to arrive at Karachi on or about 7 May.[1]

On 8 May, MacLaren wrote a complimentary statement from Drigh Road, Karachi:

Owing to the hospitality of the Maharajah of Jodhpur, we are very comfortably settled in at Parlu, and the machine is partially protected with tarpaulins. It is attached to sleepers and rails supplied by the Jodhpur–Bikaner Railway. An aerodrome has been specially prepared for our departure.

A new engine from Baghdad arrived at Karachi to-day, and will be despatched to-morrow morning in order to arrive at Parlu early on the morning of May 10th. With luck the machine should be ready the same night, and we should leave on the following morning, via Jodhpur, for Nazirabad.

It is appallingly hot and there have been many sandstorms. The hull of the machine is swathed in tarpaulin bandages and two men are employed all day throwing water on it from a deep well, which is fortunately near. The crew are all well and ready for further action.

At last the new engine arrived from Iraq Command and was brought overland on a bullock cart to the crew.

This was then fitted to the machine but it was also discovered that the tropical radiator was leaking, and efforts to repair it proved unavailing. So, a start was made with an ordinary radiator, and at 0535 on 13 May they set off towards Calcutta. With a huge crowd of onlookers, they went forward on the newly cleared runway with a final farewell before turning on course for Nasirabad and then on to Allahabad.

After a two-hour flight, they landed at Nasirabad at 0730. MacLaren telegraphed:

We left Parlu 05.35, local time and arrived at Nasirabad at 07.30. The journey was uneventful. We intended to proceed to Allahabad to-day, but owing to a leaky radiator are unable to leave here until to-morrow. The machine has not suffered much from its enforced stay at Parlu. Crew all well.

Andrews made temporary repairs to the leaking radiator, and the next morning, on 14 May, they set off at 0600 in beautiful calm weather for Bamraoli Air Force Station landing ground, about six miles west of Allahabad City, arriving at noon. Here they were once again given a hearty welcome by a number of military officers and civil dignitaries. And again it was extremely hot, necessitating the machine to be parked near a well so water could again be used to avoid heat damage to the hull.

Despite making repairs to the leaking radiator at Nasirabad, it had been decided to fit a new tropical radiator, and the RAF had organised for this to be sent to Allahabad. But the radiator was delayed, and so once again they were held back from continuing their journey to Calcutta.

Both MacLaren and Plenderleith kept a log for the entire world flight, but in many instances, the timings and dates of where they were differed. This could well have been because of their fatigue and delays in making up the logs, and there may have been occasions when the airmen would hardly have known what day it was, let alone the date.

On their arrival at Dum Dum Aerodrome, eight miles from Calcutta, at 1115—probably on 16 May—MacLaren's statement to the Press, according to *The Times*, read: 'We left Allahabad according to programme, and followed the railway line; and that's all there is to be said.'

The flight had been uneventful and made in good conditions, and they were welcomed by the commanding officer of the 1st Cameron Highlanders, together with a number of RAF officers and a small group of soldiers and airmen. It was extremely hot, as it was nearing noon, and after the formalities the crew enjoyed the luxury of ice cold beers.

Meanwhile, back in England, Napiers had been arranging for a replacement low-compression engine, to replace the high-compression one, which would be dispatched overland to Marseilles on 1 May, hopefully to arrive in time to catch the P&O mail steamer *Morea*, sailing to Bombay on 3 May. It was due to arrive on 16 May for transfer to Calcutta by 21 May where the Vulture would be waiting for them. As this would mean a further five-day wait, MacLaren decided that they should not stay at Dum Dum Aerodrome but fly on to Calcutta, where they could land at Maidan recreation ground and put the Vulture under the shade of trees by the polo ground. This would also mean increased opportunity to 'fly the Vulture's flag' and ensure that everyone knew about their courageous attempt to fly round the world.

With more delays on the horizon, MacLaren, reporting to *The Times*, laid emphasis on the fact that no fault whatever had been found with the engines. All had worked splendidly, and it was only the sheerest ill luck that there had been irritating and delaying mishaps. He wanted to make quite sure that correspondents made this clear.

Four days were then spent busily installing the new engine, while the airframe was carefully checked for any further deterioration. Where necessary, parts were revarnished and instruments, cameras and cinematograph equipment cleaned. All three crew were invited to various social functions before they were finally ready to take off on the next leg of the journey.

13

Akyab to Bangkok

The Vulture left the Maidan Polo ground in Calcutta at 0530 on 21 May to the cheers of the Cameron Highlanders and an enormous crowd of well-wishers to see her on her way. The crew were now going into the tropical stage of the journey in the monsoon season and relying entirely on their own resources. This was known to be a very difficult stage of the journey across the Bay of Bengal. It was here that Major Wilfred Theodore Blake, who had made the first attempt to fly round the world in 1922, came to grief and had to cancel his attempt.

MacLaren's log read that they ran into heavy rainstorms for a great deal of the way:

08.20	Sighted the Burma Mountains in the distance; dodging rainstorms.
09.20	Arrived Cox's Bazaar; turning SSE and following coastline.
09.40	Passed Elephant Point.
09.55	Ran into another heavy rainstorm at a height of 4,200 feet.
10.00	Conditions ahead very unfavourable, rain falling in torrents
10.30	The last 30 minutes have been spent in flying through a solid sheet of water at a height of 500 feet. Could just see the sea.

10.40	Weather ahead clear. Akyab Island visible. Rain storms all around.
10.52	More rain. Sighted Akyab.
11.10	Landed on golf course.

The Vulture was once more unable to continue on the journey. There were unfavourable weather reports from the Bay of Bengal with severe cyclonic storms, torrential rain and high winds going on down to Rangoon, Burma.

However, three days later, on 24 May, Empire Day, a slight improvement in the weather allowed them to leave on their onward journey to Rangoon at 1115. But this was to be the final flight of Vulture G-EBHO.

As they took off, the difficult weather continuing, Plenderleith discovered that the aircraft was barely controllable. The undercarriage could not be retracted, so he had no choice but to bring the Vulture down into a heavy swell with the undercarriage lowered. But this was too much for the hull, which was severely damaged, and the aircraft began to sink into the waters of Akyab Harbour.

One witness clearly remembered this terrible accident. The writer Maurice Collis, who from 1923 to 1925 was Akyab's Deputy Commissioner, was living at the time in a large house affording fine views of both the ocean and the anchorage. He later recalled that he had once observed from his veranda a small aeroplane inbound from Calcutta falling into the harbour.[1]

MacLaren was to report on this disaster:

We took off from the aerodrome at Akyab at 11.05, and with difficulty cleared the tops of the trees with the engine running well, but when over the sea at 75 miles an hour, we found the machine was dropping. At 50 feet, and travelling too fast to alight on the water, we throttled down, but the machine dropped like a stone hitting the water and smashing in the bottom of the hull. The water poured in, and there was just time to get on to the tail before the nose became completely submerged. We saved only a dispatch-case. A rowing boat came to the rescue, but the machine although almost completely submerged, continued to float until it finally beached in six feet of water on a spot which is dry at low tide. The engine was undamaged. All the instruments, cameras, etc., except the compass, were completely ruined. The accident was due to the machine being waterlogged by torrential rains, causing over-expansion and sogginess after the contraction caused by the heat of the Sind desert and continual exposure to extreme conditions. I propose to wait for the spare machine from Tokyo, and then carry on with the flight. All are quite fit and are anxiously awaiting the spare machine.[2]

Their only hope of continuing with the venture now rested entirely with the spare Vulture—G-EBGO—which had been shipped out to Tokyo in packing crates at the beginning of the world flight, just in case it might be needed. Tokyo was 4,000 miles away, and the machine was still in pieces in its original packing crates. The challenge of finding suitable transportation and the huge time delay involved meant this might have been the end of the venture.

However, while in Calcutta on 15 May, MacLaren had been informed that Lieutenant Colonel Broome, who was in charge of the arrangements for the flight across the Pacific, had arrived in Tokyo with the Canadian Navy trawler HMCS *Thiepval*, having laid down many of the supply bases which were needed by the Vulture and their crew for the North Pacific route.

Broome had already met up with the American flyers attempting to fly round the world in the opposite direction, as they had previously arrived in Tokyo. As it happened, the news of the Vulture's crash was received by telegram on 25 May while Broome was having breakfast with the leader of the American expedition, Lieutenant Smith, in the Imperial Hotel. Smith immediately contacted Commander Abbot of the United States navy, who was also there in the hotel, and he offered to transport the British machine in one of their destroyers which was to come from Yokohama to Hakodate (Tokyo), then to Hong Kong and on to Akyab.

So, despite the fact that the Americans were in direct competition with the British flyers in their desire to fly round the world, they gave every assistance in the fastest way possible, to help MacLaren continue the journey. *The Times* was to report: 'This sporting offer to assist a friendly rival is very much appreciated by the organizers of the British world flight here.'[3]

Broome was also to write a letter to the editor of *The Times* from Tokyo, dated 5 July 1924, telling the story of what happened:

Sir, I hope this letter will reach you before the American Round-the-World Flight alights on English soil, for I have a pleasant tale to tell.

One Sunday morning, May 25 of this year to be exact, I was having breakfast in the bedroom of the leader of the flight, Lieutenant Smith, in the Imperial Hotel, Tokyo. This was arranged so that we could be free from interruption and talk flying shop and swap experiences to our hearts content. For Lieutenant Smith and the stout lads with him had just flown the Pacific Ocean for the first time in history, and I had preceded him over the same route by a few weeks in a rusty, fussy little trawler laying Major MacLaren's dumps. In the rooms I found a merry tousle-headed party, running in and out of the bedroom in various stages of undress and getting into their uniforms in readiness for the day's engagements. For Japan was pouring out the splendid hospitality of the East, and was delighting in doing them honour for their great feat. We ordered grapefruit, ham and eggs and coffee, and settled down to recount our several adventures since we all last met on Langley Flying Field in Virginia the previous February.

These splendid lads—for I, alas, am twice as old and have a son older than the youngest of them—had just plucked a fair laurel, to wear for evermore on those rumpled heads of theirs, and had only a few short days before writing their names on the same scroll as Vitus Bering, that stout-hearted Dane over whose cold grave among the sand dunes of the Komandorskis they had flown. Does one need much imagination to picture his scurvy racked bones stirring uneasily as the three great aeroplanes roared above the time-obliterated trenches where he and 18 of his dead crew wait and wait? I think not.

Well, we laughed and chatted, and the hour for the first engagements for the day drew near, when there came a knock at the door, and I was handed a telegram: "MacLaren crashed at Akyab, Burma, plane completely wrecked—continuance of British flight doubtful." Without a word I handed it to Smith. He read it and passed it on to the others. Being but human, how could I help thinking first of my own bitter disappointment? Then I thought of MacLaren at Akyab, his beautiful machine a wreck, and how he must be thinking of the great delay in getting the aeroplane that I was loading on to the trawler in Hakodate Harbour that very day as a spare for our Pacific flight.

That and a thousand other thoughts were tumbling over each other, when Smith said, "We'll get that machine to MacLaren somehow. Come up to Commander Abbot's bedroom and talk it over." We found Commander Abbot, of the United States Navy, in his pyjamas, and within five minutes these gallant sportsmen had roughed out practicable plans how Abbot would rush one of his destroyers to Hakodate and load and carry the huge cases as far as Nagasaki, where his beat, so to speak, ended, meanwhile wirelessing his admiral for permission to take it further, all the way to Akyab if necessary. I left them then to get off a cable to our Commander-in-Chief of the China station asking if he could assist?

Within a few hours an answer came from Admiral Washington, commanding the American Asiatic Fleet, offering to transport our machine all the 5,000 miles to Akyab at full speed. As hours were precious, and no answer had arrived from our Commander-in-Chief, I gladly accepted Admiral Washington's offer on MacLaren's behalf, and that same evening the U.S. destroyer *John Paul Jones* left for Hakodate at 25 knots. Two days later I was informed that our Commander-in-Chief regretted that he had no vessel available.

I had at once cabled MacLaren the good news and got a cable in reply of just two words, "Well done". It was addressed to me, whereas it should have been addressed to our great-hearted fellow aviators—not our rivals or opponents, but our very gallant friends. I also cabled to the great firm of Vickers, who had built our plane, and they answered, "Please tender to American naval authorities our thanks for a very kind action." I called on the American Ambassador in Japan and cabled to Admiral Washington, but the spoken or written word cannot convey the gratitude due for what will always remain a wonderful memory—instantaneous help and sympathy in our ill-luck, the first prompt and practical, and the second as tender as it was welcome. So I can only repeat and hand on MacLaren's message, "Well done."

I am, etc., L. E. Broome, Lt. Col.[4]

The USS *John Paul Jones* left Yokahama for Hakodate at 0700 on 28 May, arriving the following evening. The Vulture, in her packing crates, was loaded and they left the next day for Hong Kong, where they were due to arrive on 2 June. The plane would then be placed on another American destroyer bound for Akyab, which it hoped to reach on 7 June.

A cable was sent to MacLaren by Broome with all the information:

Spare machine left May 29 on USS John Paul Jones, due Hong Kong 0800, June 2, will transship to another American destroyer same day and leave for Akyab direct. If weather favourable should reach you June 7. Our own China Squadron unable to assist. This splendid prompt, and sporting act is the free gift of America.

But it was not until eighteen days later, on 12 June, that the USS *William B. Preston* arrived in Akyab harbour. Most of the packing crates were unloaded onto the jetty, but some of the larger cases had to be craned off onto lighters in order to bring them ashore. They were then taken to a temporary aeroplane shed, where it took Andrews a week to construct the machine with the help of the American destroyer's crew.

All this time the monsoon weather continued relentlessly, and it was not until 21 June that MacLaren was able to report to *The Times*:

The new machine is all ready for departure, but we are unable to make a test owing to the unceasing torrential rains. The rainfall here is stupendous: I have never seen the like before. The machine is housed in a temporary bamboo and leaf shed on the Maidan, and is partially protected from the elements. We propose to test the machine on the first available opportunity, and if all is right to leave at once for Rangoon.[5]

Plenderleith's log read: 'Machine replaced by G-EBGO but another month wasted. What a different machine. Absolutely O.K.'

A month after the crash at 0855 on 25 June, they finally lifted off from Akyab Aerodrome, flying south down the coast to Rangoon. Despite it only being overcast with a light easterly wind, the weather prospects were not looking good. They soon flew back into heavy monsoon rains. Bad visibility forced them to put down at a place called Kyaing Creek at 1110.

Then, at 1250, they heard the sound of aeroplane engines and spotted the American expedition's three Douglas World Cruisers overhead—flying the other way and quite oblivious to the Vulture below. MacLaren expressed regret in not being able to meet them at some stage of their journeys, as he would have liked to have thanked them personally for their wonderful help in Tokyo. It would also have been an opportunity to obtain a few hints about the journey across the Pacific.

An hour and twenty minutes later, at 1310, they took off once again in steady rain. However, at 1345 the rain had stopped, and a few minutes later they saw their first patch of sky for a fortnight. They turned inland and were soon running into torrential rain with bad visibility once again, so they turned back to the coast. They managed to scrape in over the mountain tops, and to their great relief they were safely through.

Crossing the Bassein and Irrawady Rivers, they now realised they were running short of petrol and at 1630 landed on the water at Yandoon to refuel. They were airborne again at 1737 and finally arrived at Rangoon Harbour at 1815—nearly five hours later than planned. They were lucky to find a landing place, as the light was failing; although very tired, the airmen were reported to be fit.

It was here that MacLaren decided to reduce the Vulture's load by leaving behind all non-essential items in order to counter the adversities of flying through the tropics in the monsoon season, reducing their weight from 7,000 to around 6,500 lbs.

Two days later, on 27 June, they took off from Monkey Point bound for Bangkok. The weather that morning dawned fine and a large gathering watched their departure to bid them farewell. The Vulture rose beautifully into the morning air and circled round a couple of times over the waving crowds before finally turning south-east towards Bangkok.

14

Rangoon to Tokyo

There was no doubt that the weather conditions for this particular part of the flight were to cause a great deal of difficulty and fear.

As the Vulture flew off from Rangoon on the way to Bangkok, they headed in a southerly direction inland to cross the Bilauktaung Range on the border of Thailand. The weather was closing in on them once again with very low clouds over the mountains and storms getting worse, meaning they were compelled to fly at a height of 100 ft. As they approached the mountains, they miraculously escaped crashing into the rocky sides due to Plenderleith's superb reactions and flying skill in handling the machine.

MacLaren later reported: 'The machine was buffeted about like a cork in a torrent!'

It was quite impossible to continue, so the airmen diverted back to Tavoy, the deep-sea port of Burma, and anchored in the river to stay the night.

An entry in the log read: 'Landed at Tavoy owing to filthy weather. Filled up with petrol scrounged from two Ford cars.' They never missed an opportunity for getting help when it was needed!

They left Tavoy at 1155 on 28 June and, although there was still low cloud and storms, they managed to squeeze through two mountain tops and then were flying over sheer jungle. They sighted the Tenasserim River and followed it through the next range of mountains into another jungle valley, cleared the last range of mountains and were once more over a vast stretch of jungle with no let-up in the weather conditions. But they fortunately landed safely at Don Mueang

Aerodrome in Bangkok at 1355 and all the crew were very tired but relieved.

MacLaren proposed to leave for Haiphong in Vietnam early the next day. In turn, they spent the time refuelling and giving the machine a thorough check-over, as the weather was still proving to be very adverse, then a few hours of rest, so that they were in the right spirits to set off again.

On 29 June they left at 0607 in calm but cloudy weather, although with a favourable wind. However, they were once again to experience very difficult conditions. They followed the Mekong river northwards to Thakhek and flew up to 7,000 ft to clear the mountains tops, which were still in thick cloud. They were unable to see anything below and were a little afraid to go above the clouds for fear of trouble during a possible forced landing. They then decided to drop through the clouds to negotiate the mountains from below the cloud level. Dropping down through a hole in the clouds, they found that their plight was worse because the mountain tops were obscured and they had to fly about 100 ft above long grass in a swampy jungle. They then attempted to find a jungle clearing with the intention of landing and waiting for better weather conditions. But by then, flying at a height of only 10 ft, Plenderleith instinctively knew that if they did land, they would probably not be able to take off again. Instead, he managed to climb to 9,000 ft where they once again found the sky.

MacLaren's log read:

That little experience took about 10 years off our lives. We were never so frightened before. While we were down over the jungle, we saw a large herd of elephants and another of buffaloes, and any amount of deer. It is wonderful shooting country and if we get around safely we would like to return there for some sport!

MacLaren then set a rough compass course for Vinh in Vietnam, and about an hour later they dropped down again over the jungle and finally sighted the sea and the city of Vinh, where they landed at 1245. They needed to refuel once again, the aircraft's fuel reserves having been greatly reduced due to the time taken to fly over the mountains. With another 150 miles between them and Haiphong, it was imperative to keep the tanks topped up.

Their arrival was not expected, so there was nobody to receive them. MacLaren and Plenderleith went inshore to search for petrol and oil, which they duly found, much to their delight.

They resumed their flight at 1550 and followed the coast, although they still encountered severe storms and some very unpleasant and bumpy conditions before finally landing at Haiphong, Vietnam at 1805.

MacLaren's log read: One of the longest days and certainly worst experiences of the flight—whole trip was over nine hours.

Once again, nobody was expecting them, as it was a Sunday and the telegraph office was closed. They could not obtain petrol or oil that night so had to wait until the next day. They did manage to contact the British consulate and were invited to stay as their guests overnight, which was greatly appreciated, since they were exhausted.

The next day, 30 June, they returned to the machine straight away to refuel and complete the routine checks. They managed to leave Haiphong at 1010 in dead calm weather, although the Vulture had difficulty taking off in the still air. They were now on their way to Hong Kong.

The weather did not remain calm, though, and rain began to fall, turning into some heavy storms as they travelled east towards Pak-Hoi, China, causing them to descend to 1,000 ft. They passed Macao at 1555, finally reaching Hong Kong at 1712, where they alighted beautifully on the water behind Stonecutters Island, about three miles from the city.

By the time they reached Hong Kong, the replacement Vulture had completed a total of over 2,000 miles and thirty-one hours' flying time, much of it in appalling weather conditions.

They were given the most hearty reception from a crowded fleet of launches, including Sir Reginald Edward Stubbs, the governor. The Vulture had already received a great deal of publicity earlier in the month when the USS *John Paul Jones* had arrived in Hong Kong with the packing crates containing G-EBGO for onward transfer to Akyab. Now everyone could see the new Vulture in its full glory. That evening, the crew were the guests of the East Surrey Regiment, and the next day

MacLaren and Plenderleith were entertained for 'tiffin' at the Hong Kong Club and later dined at Government House.

Also there was the French pilot Lieutenant Pelletier d'Oisy (nickname 'Roly Poly'), who had also been attempting a world flight. However, his endeavour had already come to an end, and *The Times* reported that he was on his way to Indochina to shoot big game before returning to France.[1]

Some much-needed rest was enjoyed on their second day, and Andrews once again gave the machine a thorough service check before their departure. There were still 800 miles to go to Shanghai, with an overnight stop planned at Foochow.

On 2 July at 0930, they once again took to the air and witnessed a large gathering of launches and small boats to see them off. They were now en route for Foochow, heading along the coast towards the Formosa Strait, and the weather proved to be very kind to them.

They had an excellent flight and landed at the Pagoda Anchorage at Foochow at 1645. Here they once again refuelled and checked the aircraft and found that a propeller blade was badly chipped. It was suggested that the cause may perhaps have been a loose nut that had flown out from the engine casing, but the damage was soon repaired with great help from the Chinese authorities.

They stayed overnight and left for Shanghai at 0700 on 3 July. In perfect weather, they followed the coast to Hangzhou Bay before flying across country and landing on the Bund, Shanghai at 1540. Arrangements for their landing had been made by the Asiatic Petroleum Company assisted by former members of the RAF.

Unfortunately, Andrews was by now suffering from heatstroke and had a temperature of 105°F. He had started to feel unwell in Hong Kong while he was working on the machine and then had slept all the way from Foochow. He was immediately taken to hospital on arrival at Shanghai. It was decided that MacLaren and Plenderleith would continue the journey to Japan, with Andrews following by sea and rejoining them as soon as he could.

In the meantime, MacLaren and Plenderleith were invited to lunch at the Shanghai Club by the British members and later dined there as guests of former members of the RAF. They were also greeted by General Sheng, commander of the Chinese air force. The next day being 4 July, they joined the American community at their country club for their Independence Day celebrations and dance.

On 5 July, they continued their journey to Tokyo, where they planned to replace the engine again in readiness for the most difficult section of the route. They took off from Shanghai at 1010 and it was reported that they arrived at Kogoshima, a tiny seaport on the southern tip of Japan, at 1700, after a flight of six hours and fifty minutes in beautiful weather. They were met with dignified respect by a small local population as news of their arrival had already been sent ahead.

They spent the night there and then took off the next morning at 0750 with a short stop planned to refuel and refresh at Kushimoto. Flight Lieutenant Bryant (who was attached to the British Embassy in Tokyo as language officer) was also flying with them to Kasumigaura, until Andrews was able to rejoin them. Bryant had been requested by the embassy to organise the arrangements for the passage of the Vulture across Japan.

At this stage MacLaren was piloting the plane, and he became aware that they were once again short of petrol some miles before Kushimoto. His log read:

We had planned to fly without a stop to Kushimoto, but dense fog prevented us from following the intended course and made me steer most carefully to avert any possible danger of dashing into mountains or cliffs. We were compelled to fly back to Kagoshima and to take a roundabout route, off the headland of Sata, which lengthened my course by over 100 miles. The flight was made at an altitude varying from 300ft. to 1000ft. Lack of petrol forced us to stop at Susami for a fresh supply.

They still received great help, and at 1350 the Japanese battleship IJN *Asahi* sent an aeroplane to the town of Susami heavily laden with the necessary cans of petrol on board. Unfortunately, this aircraft crashed as it landed, but luckily the Japanese pilot, Iguchi, was only slightly injured, and the cans of petrol came to no harm.

So, after refuelling, MacLaren was able to resume the flight to Kushimoto, landing safely at 1708. Although they were three hours overdue, they were given a very warm welcome by the authorities and local citizens. There were also many school children there in smart uniforms patiently waiting and holding Union Jacks to greet the airmen. MacLaren expressed his great appreciation for all that had been done to make them welcome, and for the assistance given to them that day by the *Asahi,* and sympathetically referred to the injuries sustained by the pilot whilst responding to their predicament.

MacLaren and his crew stayed at Kushimoto overnight, and at 0954 the next morning, 7 July, they were on their way again heading for Tokyo.

After a good flight, they arrived at Kasumigaura Naval Air Station, Tokyo and the many people who had undertaken the four-hour journey from their homes the previous day were rewarded by the sight of the Vulture arriving in perfect weather conditions at 1440, albeit three hours overdue. There were once again many school children there dressed in their 'Sunday best' and waving Japanese and British flags.

Many dignitaries turned out to greet them, including Admiral Komatsu, commanding the air station; Commander Hara, representing the Japanese navy; Engineer Captain Hayashi, Lieutenant Miki, Admiral Itami, Vickers' representative in Japan; Captain Royle, the British naval attaché representing the ambassador; Mr A. P. Scott of the Rising Sun Petroleum Company; Colonel Obata, representing the Japanese Army; Captain Uno, representing the Imperial Aerial Society; Major Chichester-Smith, Colonel Orde-Lees, Flight Lieutenant Bryant, attached to His Majesty's Embassy as language officer, and of course Colonel Broome, who had organised delivery of the Vulture G-EBGO to MacLaren in Akyab and was now going to join them on the next leg of the journey.

Admiral Komatsu made a speech in which he said:

Our naval aviation owes much to the Royal Air Force. In particular this air station was brought to perfection from its infancy by the efforts of Colonel the Master of Sempill and the officers under him, work which is always gratefully remembered by our nation and increases our welcome to you on this aerodrome, where the British

Air Mission's efforts are firmly planted. After the old custom on a Samurai's triumphant arrival, we drink to your health and good luck in the final achievement.

Admiral Itami added: 'I am sure that British traditions will win through.'

But this was not how Commander Hara was to understand the British undertaking. At this time, Commander Hara had been working hard for the Imperial Japanese Navy (IJN) to acquire British planes. However, only weeks later he was strongly critical of the Vickers Vulture, calling it an 'unsuitable machine', due to not only the flight's final failure, but also 'the chain of misadventures which preceded it.' He now considered that the IJN would favour French and German aircraft instead.

But before these considerations were to emerge, MacLaren said in his speech that he and his party had been given a welcome greater than they deserved and that he hoped that his visit would have a good effect on Anglo-Japanese relations. He also paid great respect and gave thanks for all the help that the Japanese had given them at Kagoshima and Kushimoto. He went on to say that he was thankful to have reached Japan safely and that now with half his flight around the world accomplished, he was confidently looking forward to the Kurils stage, so splendidly reconnoitred by Colonel Broome.

He also remarked that a great deal of gratitude was owed to the Americans, for without their help in getting his spare machine to Akyab, he would have been unable to continue. He added that the aeroplane and engine were performing very well and while they were at the Naval Air Station, he planned to give the Vulture a thorough overhaul in readiness for their next stage. The wings were to be given another two coats of varnish, and the engine given a major service. In conclusion he again expressed his appreciation and went on to say how greatly impressed he was by the warmth of the Japanese welcome.

By this time Andrews had fortunately recovered and he rejoined them at the Air Station the following day, 8 July, where they were guests of the squadron pilots. The crew were now once again made to feel very honoured. They were taken to a luncheon given in their honour at the Imperial Hotel by Tsuyoshi Inugai, the minister of communications, and had four rooms and four motor cars placed at their disposal. Most of the senior government ministers were present including Viscount Kato, the prime minister; General Ugaki, minister of war; Admiral Takarabi, minister of marine; and their vice ministers; Baron Sakatani and General Nagaoka, vice-presidents of the Imperial Aerial Society.

They were all presented with the Imperial Aerial Society Gold Medal, specially designed and made by Mitsukoshi to commemorate the occasion. They were also each given an inscribed silver rose bowl and went to receptions at the Imperial University and the Maple Club.

They had now completed 10,770 miles since leaving Southampton and with 12,484 miles still to go, MacLaren was very keen to be on their way again. From here they would be taking Colonel Broome with them to help navigate and locate the supply dumps that he had provided throughout the chain of islands en route to Alaska. Now a crew of four, Broome was to join Andrews in the bow cockpit. This extra weight meant a great deal of reorganisation needed to be done, requiring them to offload all but essential equipment. As this included leaving behind the wheels and undercarriage, they were now committed to water landings exclusively.

The flying programme was now to be broken into the following stages:

July 12   Kasumigaura to Minato
July 13   Minato to Kushiro
July 14   Kushiro to Hitokatpu
July 15   Hitokatpu to Broughton Bay; then on to Paramushir,
             weather permitting.

With all this done, they took off five days later, on 12 July. They would now be flying over northern Japan before heading off up the Kuril Islands to the Kamchatka Peninsula and across the International Date Line to Alaska. This was one of the hardest parts of the journey, as they would be flying over a long chain of isolated and mostly uninhabited volcanic islands where the terrain was desolate and fog-infested. There was also a great risk of running into flocks of large, slow-moving birds which could easily break the propeller.

These were the 'smoky seas' of which Kipling wrote in 'The Rhyme of the Three Sealers':

The weeping fog rolled fold on fold, the wrath of man to cloak,
Half-steam ahead by guess and lead, for the sun is mostly veiled—
Through fog to fog, by luck and log, sail ye as Bering sailed;[2]

But with the constant courage and dedication of the crew of the Vulture, and MacLaren's adventurous spirit and need to get on with the endeavour, they continued in brave and gallant spirits.

At that time, *The Times* was to report:

With their task about half completed, Squadron Leader MacLaren, Flying Officer Plenderleith and Sergeant Andrews have shown that—given this spirit of cooperation among airmen of different nations and a proper distribution of spare parts, engines, machines and aerodromes along the route—there is practically no limit to the length of air-voyages, which may be undertaken with success even by single aeroplanes or seaplanes, unsupported by others, and forced, during the greater part of their flight, to rely entirely on their own initiative and resource. The day when the navigation of the air will be as safe and as sure a means of transport as any other devised by the mind and hand of man has been brought sensibly nearer.[3]

Tokyo to Alaska

The Vulture was now heading north for the Japanese city of Minato, but once again they were delayed and had to return to Kasumigaura for repairs to a leaking radiator.

The log here is a little unclear as to dates and places of landing, but *The Times* was to report that they set off again on 13 July and arrived at Minato at 1800 after a terrible journey of twelve hours through thick fog. Visibility had been so bad that they had to risk two forced landings on the way, rather than continue flying on almost blind.

On 14 July they left early in the morning and made a flight of three hours and fifteen minutes to Kushiro, on the south-east coast of the island of Yezo (Hokkaido). It was now better weather and they just stopped for a short break before continuing on their way at 1300, heading for Hitokatpu Bay in the Kuril Islands.

MacLaren sent a telegraph from Minato:

Leaving Japan to-day along the complete chain of petrol dumps, many of which are in unexplored regions, arranged by Lieutenant-Colonel Broome with the assistance of the Rising Sun Petroleum Company, which spared no expense or trouble for our success. If we are unsuccessful the organisation is not to blame.

The next report to the newspapers signalled that they had landed at Toshimoi on the east coast of Yeterufu (Staaten Island), the first of the

Kuril Islands, at 1500. Although they had arrived in good weather, by the next morning the visibility had changed to only a few yards. They had no idea how long it would take for the fog to lift. The only way of getting a weather report would have been to contact ships in the area, but with no wireless facilities they just had to sit it out.

They were able to set off again at 0740 on 15 July, as the fog had cleared a little, but the next few days brought some alarming newspaper headlines.

Reuters reported that on 16 July MacLaren was six hours overdue at Paramushir, a volcanic island in the northern portion of the Kuril Islands, and that Japanese destroyers had been sent out to search for him.

On 17 July, *Reuters* reported that the destroyers had not yet found any trace of the machine and that the weather was cloudy but without wind. British officials thought they may have landed in Broughton Bay, Shimushiru Island, halfway between Yeterufu and Paramushir, where Broome had laid a supply base in case of necessity.

MacLaren's family at home were naturally very concerned as to what had happened and very agitated as they waited for news. By a strange coincidence, the American flyers attempting the world flight in the other direction arrived at the same time at Croydon Airport in England. Despite her concerns, MacLaren's wife Amanda made the effort to welcome, congratulate and thank them for their splendid help when the Vulture had been wrecked at Akyab.

On 17 July, The *Daily Chronicle* was to report:

One of the most interested visitors was Mrs MacLaren, the wife of the leader of the British world flight, who had very sportingly come specially to Croydon to congratulate the Americans on their success so far, and she early took the opportunity to thank Lieutenant Lowell Smith, as representing America, for the generous help given to her husband in transporting his spare machine back from Tokyo. Not without a trace of anxiety, she then inquired what they thought of Squadron leader MacLaren's chances along the Kuril Islands, and Lieutenant Lowell Smith was forced to say that Squadron Leader

MacLaren was likely to be troubled at this period of the year with very much fog.[1]

It was not until 21 July that the Japanese destroyer *Isokaze* received a message from the steamer *Urup Maru* to say that the missing aircraft had been found at Tokotan Bay, a sheltered stretch of water on the south-west shore of Urup Island. The *Isokaze* then proceeded at full speed to the island to make sure the crew and the Vulture were safe.

On arrival, everyone was found to be well and the Vulture undamaged, and MacLaren—with his usual desire to get on with the journey—was hoping to continue to Paramushir as soon as possible. A wireless message was received from MacLaren saying: 'Delayed by fog at Tokatan Bay, Urup. Will start again when weather improves. Am receiving great assistance from destroyer Isokaze.'

Newspapers were to report that through all their adventures and misadventures they had shown such a clear-headed and resourceful spirit, together with such undaunted resolution, that it was confidently hoped that they would continue to triumph over all the difficulties which may have to be faced in the remaining stages of their journey.

Back in England at their home in St John's Wood in London, Amanda was enormously relieved to hear the news and received many congratulatory messages from friends, including one from Sir Hugh Trenchard, chief of the air staff, who was godfather to their 6-year-old son, Wallace.

The *Daily Mail* reported her saying:

Oh, I am so happy! I was confident that my husband was safe... now I feel like a bird. I want to sing. My happiness is complete... and it was only young Wallace who kept me cheerful. I wish my husband were coming home, but really I wish him to go on and win through. He is a Briton, and Britons always have been wonderful; it would be only his birthright as a Britisher to be the first to conquer the air in a world flight.

But a *Daily Express* representative calling in to see Amanda noted that when she heard the news she had partly collapsed later in the day when the strain she had been suffering finally set in.

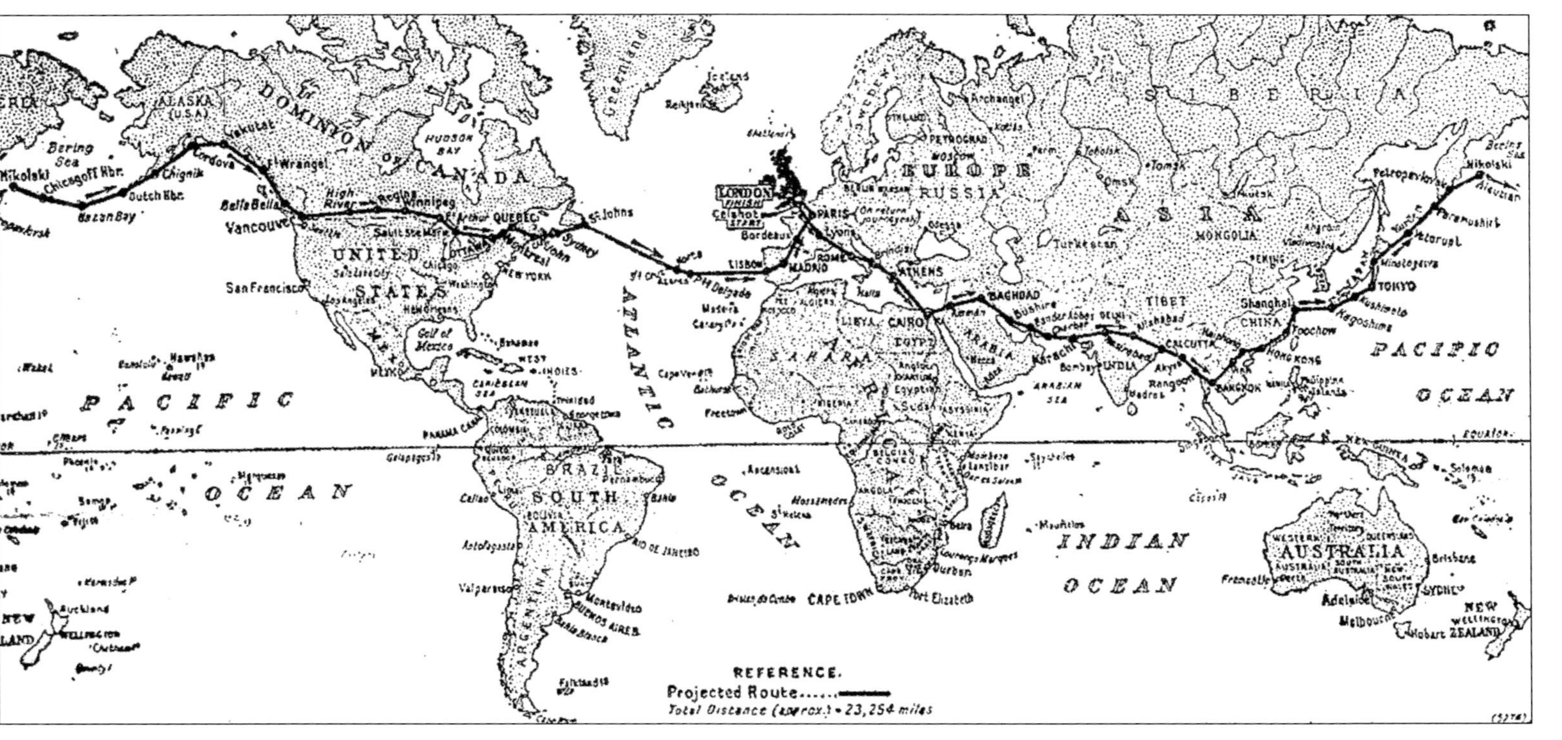

Round the world newspaper map. (*The Times*)

Left: MacLaren and his daughter Anna sitting on the nose of the Vulture. (*Shell Historical Heritage and Archive*)

Below: The Vulture taking off from the slipway at Calshot. (*Pete London collection*)

Royal Navy personnel hauling the Vulture from Lake Korrisia to the sea. (*Shelley Wilkes (née Plenderleith)*)

Installing the new engine alongside battleship HMS *Emperor of India*. (*Shelley Wilkes (née Plenderleith)*)

G-EBHO in flight. (*Shelley Wilkes (née Plenderleith*)

The Vulture with the biscuit tin being handed back. (*RAF Museum, Hendon*)

Above: The Vulture at RAF Aerodrome Hinaidi. (*Joseph Edward Cape, Hinaidi*)

Right: Guarding the Vulture in the Sind desert. (*Shelley Wilkes (née Plenderleith)*)

Delivery of the new engine across the Sind desert. (*Shelley Wilkes (née Plenderleith)*)

The Vulture resting in the shade at the Maidan recreation ground, Calcutta. (*Shelley Wilkes (née Plenderleith)*)

The atrocious rain at Akyab, 1924. (*Shelley Wilkes (née Plenderleith)*)

G-EBGO in packing crate—Akyab Harbour. (*Shelley Wilkes (née Plenderleith)*)

Constructing G-EBGO. (*Shelley Wilkes (née Plenderleith)*)

The Vulture alighting on the water behind Stonecutters Island. (*Henry Ching*)

Right: Plenderleith and MacLaren topping up fuel. (*Shell Historical Heritage & Archive, the Hague*)

Below: The crew arriving at Shanghai. (*Shell Historical Heritage & Archive*)

Above: Amanda congratulating Lieutenant Lowell Smith at Croydon. (*The British Newspaper Archive*)

Left: Anna and Wallace delighted that their father is safe. (*MacLaren family photo*)

The *Thiepval* crew welcoming Plenderleith, Andrews and Broome. (*George Metcalf Archives Collection—Canadian War Museum*)

The Vulture beached on Bering Island. (*George Metcalf Archives Collection—Canadian War Museum*)

Above: The hull of G-EBGO loaded onto HMCS *Thiepval*. (*The Virtual Maritime Museum of British Columbia, photo P2855*)

Left: The Vulture's propellor at Esquimalt naval barracks. (*Canadian Forces Base, Esquimalt, British Columbia*)

Archibald, Ethel and Anna in Florence. (*MacLaren family photo*)

Archibald outside Red Roofs. (*MacLaren family photo*)

Sketch by Wallace of his father. (*MacLaren family photo*)

Archibald in Madeira. (*MacLaren family photo*)

Squadron Leader Archibald Stuart Charles Stuart-MacLaren. (*Shell Historical Heritage and Archive*)

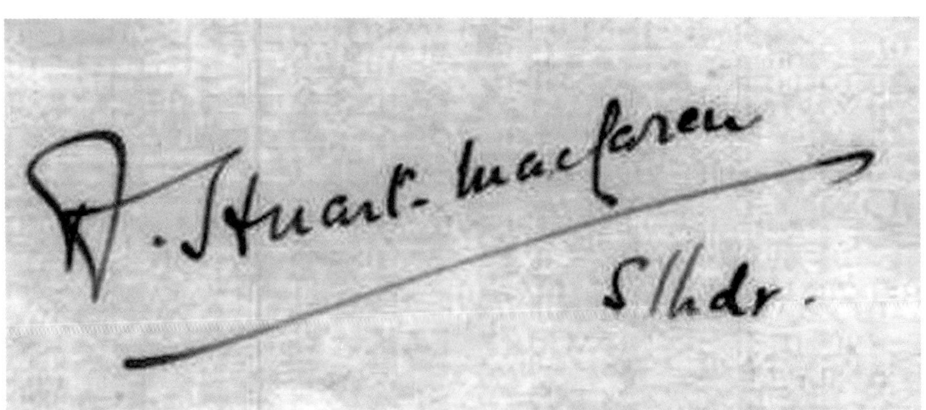

Squadron Leader Archibald Stuart-MacLaren's signature. (*MacLaren family photo*)

Young Wallace was to echo his father's adventurous spirit by saying: 'I knew Daddy was perfectly safe, and when I grow up I'm going to fly round the world too!'[2]

A British newspaper was full of admiration for what had happened and reported:

A great thrill spread through the country yesterday when it was learned that Squadron Leader MacLaren had been rescued. In the war heroism was commonplace. The wildest adventure became routine. Now in these softer times of peace we see an airman like MacLaren in a setting of romance made possible by the return of the rest of us to occupations which are harrowing enough but lack the element of personal danger and glory. MacLaren stands out, an adventurer in a period of economic reconstruction. We recognise in him a direct descendent of those dashing fellows who set sail in good Queen Bess' glorious days and annexed the seas of the world to these little islands. Therefore we rejoice at the airman's escape from death, and we specially rejoice with his wife who bravely waved him goodbye as he voyaged into the skies and who never lost faith even when the mists of the Pacific blotted out all news for so many hours.[3]

On 21 July, *The New York Times* was also to make a very positive report on the difficulties that MacLaren and his crew had experienced:

The discovery that Squadron Leader MacLaren is safe has been received in the United States with hardly less enthusiasm than if it had been one of the United States round the world pilots who had been lost and then found. MacLaren, like the American round the world flyers, was engaged at the risk of his own life in a work which will be a great benefit not only to people now living but to the generations to come. It will be therefore a matter of general rejoicing that MacLaren, who was given up for lost, has landed safely in the Kuriles and is continuing his flight. In America, which is represented in the world flight by three men who have already crossed the Pacific, Asia and Europe and are now making ready to fly home, the news of MacLaren's safety will especially be welcomed.

MacLaren was now able to send a detailed wireless message from the *Isokaze* explaining what had happened to them. They had left Yeterufu Island on 16 July and about an hour and a half later had once again run into dense fog and low cloud. They then decided to put down in Tokotan Bay, just offshore, but the wind was still coming in from the open sea and causing them great concern.

Broome had discovered that there was a small fox farm on the island, occupied by three islanders, and as he checked his charts, he was able to confirm the location of a small volcanic lake some short distance inland. As the weather was still deteriorating, it was decided that for the safety of the Vulture, they needed to make a transfer there while it was still possible. Plenderleith brought them safely into the calmer waters of the lake.

But the wind was still increasing to gale force nine, and they could not take any further chances. Plenderleith and Andrews used spikes, mooring lines and two anchors until they were fully satisfied that they could be safe overnight. At the same time, MacLaren and Broome were getting a tent pitched on the lakeside for the night but were not worried about food, as they had four days' emergency rations.

The weather remained appalling all through the night, with gale-force winds and drenching rain. So, with their tent being completely washed out, they had managed to move into a wooden hut at a small fox farm on the island where, with the benefit of a large iron stove, they were able to dry out again and sleep late into the afternoon. But within a day or two, Plenderleith had developed a very bad fever and was running a temperature of 102.3 degrees. The Vulture's log read: Got fever and passed out for a week. Flies awful.[4]

For the rest of their stay at Urup, the *Isokaze* kept them well supplied with provisions and the fox farmers provided them with very good fresh salmon. The ship's doctor took good care of Plenderleith.

The Times reported:

The other members of Squadron-Leader MacLaren's party are testing the camp equipment on the beach near the farm. Dense fog still prevails and a half-gale is blowing.

The party is in excellent spirits. Lieutenant-Colonel Broome is especially happy in his work as cook, and is proving the suitability of camp gear. Ample food and drink has been supplied from the destroyer.[5]

The Times also reported that there was a great deal of American sympathy for Squadron Leader MacLaren.

The New York Times reported on this difficult position for the British round the world flight, as opposed to their own American flyers:

The risk of MacLaren and his mechanic has been the greater because his enterprise did not have the practical support of the Air Ministry and was not carefully arranged. It is no reflection upon the skill and courage of Lieutenant Smith and his command to say that MacLaren's attempt to cross the Pacific will be the greater personal triumph if he succeeds. He seems to be taking desperate chances. If he gets away safely from the last of the Kurils he must still face the storm breeding Aleutians. [...] It was a relief to learn that the gallant Englishman has escaped disaster in those two days of mystery when he was reported to be missing in treacherous waters. Americans naturally want their own country to make the circuit of the world, but also they would like to see MacLaren carry on and prove a good second.[6]

It was now 22 July and the weather began to improve with clearer conditions to the north. Plenderleith had fortunately recovered from his fever; MacLaren made the decision to leave the following day. HMCS *Thiepval* had returned to Petropavlovsk, by the Pacific Ocean, with a spare engine on board to await their arrival.

This was the Canadian Government vessel on which Broome had been making preparations for the trans-Pacific stage of the flight. He had carried with him specially made tin-lined cases filled with rations, candles, soap, cooking utensils and general purpose knives. He also carried large drums fitted up as marking buoys to be moored in lonely harbours never entered except by an occasional native on a fishing trip. Large quantities of gasoline and oil were also carried, and great help had been given to Broome, earlier on, by the United States Air Service in Washington.

The mass of information compiled about the northern islands had been incorporated in a unique chart covering the whole flight from Tokyo to Vancouver. Furled on narrow rollers, it was by far the most important item in the equipment which had been assembled for this Pacific part of the flight.

So, at 0740 on 23 July, they set off for Paramushir in the northern Kuril Islands via Broughton Bay followed by the Japanese destroyer *Isokaze*, which was watching out for them.

Although they had no problems with weather, Plenderleith was to record: 'Urup to Broughton Bay, 2 hours 10 minutes, over clouds. A very bleak, nasty and stormy place. Reindeers blown over the cliffs into the sea.'[7] Having arrived at Broughton Bay at about 0950 they then left for Paramushir on the same day and arrived four hours later.

The next day MacLaren sent a wireless message saying:

Left Paramushir 08.30., Thursday 24th. Encountered thick fog; compelled to return 09.30. Restarted 15.10.; reached Petropavlovsk 19.35. Proceeding North Kamchatka to-morrow, Friday 25th. Sergeant Andrews ill; temperature 104 degrees. Enthusiastic meeting here with Thiepval; champagne flowing freely; everything in the garden lovely.

Later another message was sent saying simply: 'Andrews recovering.'

Having removed the wheels and undercarriage, due to the extra weight of bringing Broome on board, they once again had to land on water. But HMCS *Thiepval* was waiting for them, which was very fortunate as the weather continued to be extremely cold with wet soaking fog, and they were forced to stay for a week.

Unfortunately the hull of the *Vulture* stoved in while making their landing, but the crew of the Canadian ship proved very useful. They dug a dry dock on the beach and their carpenter began to make good the damage to the hull. He came in for warm praise from MacLaren when the job was finished, and he declared that it was a bit of work that would have done any skilled aeroplane worker credit. However, some days were sunnier and the crew aboard *Thiepval* would probably have not seen anyone for days on end, so were glad to share some time with the British airmen.

It was not until eleven days later that they finally took off, heading for the west side of Bering Island and the Aleutians to Alaska. But little did they know what was in store.

The End of the Flight

The Vulture left West Kamchatka for Bering Island at 0900 on Monday 4 August, the weather initially hazy, but at 3,000 ft the fog started to become solid again, so they descended to 100 ft to find visibility, but this was to end catastrophically.

As they neared Bering Island, the fog dropped to the surface of the sea and was all around them. In blinding rain Plenderleith suddenly swerved and avoided hitting a cliff by a margin of about two feet. Visibility was now nil and Plenderleith made a desperate landing along the swell, but both wing tips shattered and were wrenched off. The plane swerved right round, and the fabric was torn off the lower port wing. The clock stopped at 10.55.

So ended the flight of the Vulture. They had travelled a total of 13,100 miles in 130 days with a flying time of 195 hours and fifteen minutes.

The following day MacLaren was to send a wireless message from HMCS *Thiepval* at St Paul Island to explain what had happened:

The aeroplane left West Kamchatka at 09.00., on August 4. The weather was hazy but not foggy. After passing an unnamed Cape and flying at 3,000 feet we encountered fog banks, but there was clear water visibility for the first two thirds of the 119 miles between the point of Kamchatka and the west side of Bering Island. The fog then became solid ahead, and we descended to 100 feet, finding visibility again under the fog bank.

When nearing Bering Island the fog dropped to the surface of the sea all around us. The wind was 20 miles an hour on the port quarter. With the plane travelling at 100 miles an hour 100 feet above a rough sea, in blinding rain and fog, Plenderleith swerved suddenly to avoid hitting a cliff by a margin of about two feet; the island vanishing again in seconds.

As the distance and time for Bering Island had run, there was imminent danger of dashing against the cliffs of the island, and visibility was now nil. Plenderleith made a desperate landing along the swell, but being across a short confused sea, both wing-tips were shattered and wrenched off. The plane swerved right round and the fabric was torn off the lower port wing.

My first order was for life belts, which were under Colonel Broome's seat in the forward cockpit; my next was to examine the hull, for there was no sign of taking water. There was dense fog all around... we started the engine and attempted to taxi, but it was almost impossible to steer the plane, as the wing-tips buried alternately, swerving the plane around. Broome and I spent two hours running back and forth alternately along the lower wings as the plane see-sawed and the weight of the engine threatened to capsize us. We had to stop the engine repeatedly as the cooling-water boiled, and the plane threatened to dive bodily under when the tail plunged, and as this happened the wings started to break up.

During the last desperate minutes, Broome pointed eastwards as a small patch of fog lifted. The engine was started again with difficulty, as everyone was now getting exhausted with cold and wet, Plenderleith leaving the pilot's seat to help. We saw a sandy beach ahead, about two miles off, and ran in close to the breakers. The engine was now useless with a broken sprocket... everyone jumped into the bitterly cold surf and held the plane head on to the sea. As the sea dropped we beached the plane and Plenderleith and I unloaded the gear up towards the edge of the surf.

The fog lifted and the afternoon was bright, warm, and clear. The islet first seen momentarily in the fog and which we had so narrowly escaped hitting, proved to be Sea-lion Rock, 150ft. high, seven miles north-west of Nikolski......Broome set out along the beach, having recognised our position as being Buckeye Rock. On his arrival at Nikolski two boats were manned and pulled round the coast to the plane, and rendered the greatest assistance in hauling it out of reach of the surf.

A Russian wireless operator made contact with the Thiepval immediately. She started from Petropavlovsk, and arriving at daylight next morning, took us on board. The aircraft's engine and hull were salvaged and we left for Dutch Harbour at midnight.

MacLaren also sent a message to the Air Ministry in England: 'For the sake of the Royal Air Force I am sorry I have failed, but conditions were impossible for flying.'[1]

Having arrived from Petropavlovsk on 5 August, HMCS *Thiepval* set about helping to dismantle the parts of the Vulture for loading onto the ship for the onward voyage to Vancouver. They managed to load the engine, hull and propeller, which were lashed to the deck, and together with the crew set off for Dutch Harbour at midnight.

They then entered Prince Rupert Harbour, British Columbia at 0230. But in spite of it being the middle of the night, and in driving rain, there was an outburst of cheers to greet the vessel from the Mayor of the city and councillors, veterans of the Flying Corps, army officers and women and children gathered at the dock to welcome the flyers back onto British soil and to pay tribute to their gallantry and sportsmanship. At the request of Messrs. Vickers, the hulk of the Vulture was then taken to the Canadian Air Force station at Vancouver for reshipment to England, together with the Napier engine.

To this day, the big four-bladed propeller still hangs over the mantelpiece in the wardroom of the Esquimalt Canadian Forces Naval Base with the flyers' signatures inscribed in the hub, having been presented to the mess by MacLaren in recognition of the outstanding work of HMCS *Thiepval*.

There was now a round of entertainments prepared for the airmen which included an official dinner and a dance, although this could not have been easy for them as they were totally exhausted.

MacLaren discussed the many lessons which could be learned from the flight, and also paid the highest tribute to Colonel Broome for his laying down of the dumps since leaving Tokyo:

It was a masterpiece, but we encountered impossible weather conditions. You hear fog talked of at home. I myself have flown often in fog, but the fog in the Kuriles is almost unbelievable. Day after day we never got away from it. It was absolutely impenetrable. If we had waited for fine weather, we should never have got anywhere. We simply had to plug along and take chances. In my opinion it is absolutely unfeasible to attempt to fly from Tokyo by this route in the summer months without the aid of at least two vessels as escort, for two reasons. Weather reports from ahead are essential. One vessel must be ahead to send back reports, while the second must be with the machine to receive them. So fickle is the fog that when starting it may be fine and clear, but before reaching one's destination one may find utterly impenetrable banks of fog awaiting. If only one ship acts as escort it is essential that the machine itself have a wireless receiving range of 300 to 350 miles, which means, of course, adding seriously to the weight. If you come down anywhere in the Bering Sea Archipelago without vessels at hand you have not a dog's chance. Practically the whole archipelago is uninhabited. Even if you are lucky enough to land safely you might easily die of starvation. I repeat my opinion that it is utterly foolhardy to attempt the Pacific flight without vessels as escort.[2]

An American newspaper summarised the amazing journey that the Vulture had undertaken:

The Flights That Failed:
There is something almost tragic in the news that Squadron Leader MacLaren, Flying Officer Plenderleith and Sergeant Andrews have been compelled to give up their attempted flight round the world. It seems only the other day that we announced the completion of the first half of the long and adventurous journey on which they set out at the end of March. From the very start they have had to

put up with a persistent run of bad luck, and now, on the top of all the previous mishaps which they have so cheerfully surmounted, comes a fresh and unhappily, final blow. This time there can be no going forward. The pluck that carried them through their most serious troubles in Europe and Asia—off the French coast at Havre, in Corfu, in the desert of Sind, in the sea near Akyab, and in the passage of the mountains between Bangkok and Hong Kong—is of no further avail. They have been beaten by the fog, which at the outset they foresaw would prove the chief obstacle to their success. For several days it kept them prisoners in one of the Kurile group of islands and off the coast of Kamchatka, and when at last they were able to make a start on the perilous crossing to Alaska it forced them to come down in heavy seas which definitely put their machine out of action. Fortunately they themselves escaped injury, and are safe on board the Canadian trawler Thiepval, making for Vancouver. But with the wings, floats and tail of their Vickers-Napier Vulture smashed, and with no spare parts available, the venture was clearly at an end. Nothing remained for Squadron Leader MacLaren but to send his terse message—"Shall not be able to continue flight".

In this country there will be a feeling of sincere sympathy with Lieutenant Wade and Lieutenant Ogden, the two American Army pilots, who have also been forced, almost at the same time, though at a much more advanced stage in their journey, to give up the hope of finishing their flight. They are two of the little band of "our great-hearted fellow aviators"—not our rivals or opponents, but our very "gallant friends," to whom Colonel Broome referred in the letter of grateful and graceful recognition for their timely help to Squadron Leader MacLaren which we published yesterday. The "pleasant tale" which Colonel Broome had to tell is a fine testimony to the camaraderie of the air which has been so marked a feature of these world flights. When he handed to Lieutenant Smith the telegram which conveyed the news that the British machine had crashed at Akyab and that the continuance of the flight was doubtful, the "instantaneous help and sympathy" given by the American airmen showed the very highest qualities of the spirit of true sportsmanship. If it had not been for their prompt and generous offer, and the practical way in which it was approved and backed up by the Commander of the American Asiatic Fleet, the flight of Squadron Leader MacLaren and his companions would probably have ended at Akyab in May instead of in the Pacific in August. Expression has been given more than once in these columns to the feelings of gratitude which the kindly thought of Lieutenant Smith and the other American pilots aroused in the minds of the British public and the members of the Royal Air Force. But just now, when, like our own men, two of their number are smarting under a sense of bitter disappointment, Colonel Broome's letter comes as a welcome and timely reminder of what he calls that "wonderful memory". Everyone here will join in hoping that the other American machines will successfully accomplish the last lap of their flight round the world. Everyone too, will keenly sympathise with those, American as well as British, who, to use the word chosen by Squadron Leader MacLaren, have failed. They have only failed—if it can be accounted a failure—because luck was not with them. Everything that they themselves could do they have done. All alike have greatly dared and greatly accomplished, and all have a great share in the work of the peaceful development of man's supremacy in the air, which it is the object of these world flights to bring about.[3]

Time was now spent in much rest and recuperation, especially for Plenderleith and Andrews, who were still recovering from their soaring temperatures. Having now arrived at Vancouver Harbour, MacLaren avoided the crowds and motored to the city. He later joined his crew, and they all received an official address of welcome at a dinner given by the Canadian air force officers.

MacLaren told his story to reporters of his first visit to Vancouver in 1911:

Of course, I was flat broke most of the time, he said cheerfully, but I know of no country where one can have a better time on less money. I landed here in 1911 with rather less than $25 in my pocket—and no job. Not being a startling success as the budding business man in England—my people thought I would be the very thing for the west—so I came, I saw, and—I got a job as timekeeper—and enjoyed every minute of it. The contrast of my first arrival here 13 years ago, and the wonderful welcome I am now receiving here—well, it's rather overwhelming, you know. It's wonderful to me that since we did not make the grade, so to speak—the people still take any interest in us.

I feel I cannot say enough in appreciation of the splendid way Canada has helped us. The warmth of our welcome here only adds to the obligations of myself and my companions to the dominions.[4]

Many days passed. They made the journey on the Canadian national railway to Winnipeg, arriving at noon. More than a thousand people crowded the station platform and leaders in provincial, civil and military life were on hand to greet MacLaren and his party when they stepped from the platform onto the station concourse. Princess Patricia's Canadian Light Infantry Band struck a lively air and scores of spectators joined the cheer of welcome. A luncheon was then given at The Canadian Club, where MacLaren, Plendeith and Andrews were guests of honour.

While staying at the Fort Garry Hotel in Winnipeg, MacLaren was asked if he had any intention to try another round-the-world flight:

'It's all a matter of capital,' he said. 'If the British Government would put up the money then I am only too willing to have another shot. It is a difficult matter to get money privately for such enterprises. However, if the American fliers fail in their efforts, I shall certainly do my best to get the money together by hook or crook and have one more go.'

He was of the opinion, however, that despite unfavourable weather in Greenland the Americans would successfully negotiate the trip. He wished them every success in their endeavours.[5]

Then, after more restful days, they made their way to Ottawa, where MacLaren accepted an invitation from Major B. Hobbs, the Commandant of the Victoria Beach Air Station, to spend a weekend of seclusion at the beach. Andrews made the trip to the beach by plane in high wind, then returned to Fort Garry in Winnipeg, while Plenderleith decided to remain in Manitoba.

In some of the many speeches that MacLaren made during their stay in Canada, he summarised the difficulties of their journey. He was convinced that the greatest mistake was overloading with unnecessary spares, especially at Corfu and Parlu. But he was full of praise for the third engine which was installed at Calcutta and which never misfired or needed any mechanical adjustments. The problems with the first two came from overstrain.

MacLaren considered the route to have been perfect, but that the month's delay at Akyab had ruined all their plans because if they had arrived at the Kuril Islands a month earlier, the weather would have been considerably easier. He had been absolutely satisfied that the type of machine used was the best possible and said that if he attempted the flight again, he would use the same machine. The petrol and oil from Shell were also said to be of perfect quality.

On 29 August, MacLaren, Plenderleith and Andrews set off on their homeward journey back to England on the Canadian Pacific Liner *Montclare* and finally arrived in Liverpool on 20 September.

They were greeted in Liverpool by MacLaren's wife Amanda and a small gathering of the press, after which they boarded the train to Euston Station in London for their last journey together. But this time there was no one there to greet them—no official welcome, no representatives from the Air Ministry or the Royal Aero Club, despite the words of the secretary of state for air at Calshot on 25 March when they set off: "We will promise them a splendid welcome on their return". It seemed that all the lessons learned from this extraordinary venture meant very little.

The Times reported:

PLUCKY BRITISH AIRMEN BACK IN LONDON

These men who had risked their lives in a thousand different places during their gallant attempt to circle the globe by aeroplane received a splendid send-off at Southampton a few months ago, but their return seemed not to stir any one of those officials and friends who had feted them on that occasion.

They came from Liverpool just like ordinary travellers despite the fact that their return had been mentioned in all the newspapers yesterday.[6]

There was also a letter sent to the Editor of *The Daily Mail* by a British gentleman who clearly saw the situation in a similar way:

Sir,

I think everybody will agree with your remarks regarding the lack of welcome to Squadron Leader MacLaren after his wonderful flight. It is hardly the British way to ignore a man because, battling single-handed against very great odds, he failed to achieve his object.

I do not wish to belittle the American flight in any way; it is interesting to note that the United States Air Service made arrangements with tremendous thoroughness and began real work in plotting this flight twelve months before the actual day of departure. Advance officers travelled and worked in the farthermost quarters of the earth, laying down supplies, charting courses and studying weather. In 55 arranged stops were spare engines for 6 changes of motor, complete spares for 16 Liberty motors, and 8 planes.

Did our Air Force make similar thorough preparations for MacLaren and would the Americans have got through had they only sent one machine?[7]

However, on 25 September, there was a luncheon reception given in their honour at the Hotel Cecil in London by the chairman and directors of Vickers Ltd, Napier and Son Ltd, Shell Mex Ltd and some senior dignitaries from the RAF. Unfortunately Andrews was not able to be present owing to continuing illness.

The following day, *The Times* reported:

MACLAREN'S STORY
THE WORLD FLIGHT ADVENTURE
TRIBUTE TO PLUCKY AIRMEN

Commander Sir Trevor Dawson Bt., vice chairman of Vickers Ltd. congratulated the guests on the great success they had attained. They had kept the flag of the old country flying and had shown indomitable courage in the face of great difficulties, against which it was quite impossible to provide. They congratulated them upon the work they had done, and upon having maintained the spirit and tradition of the Royal Air Force. They were happy indeed to see them home again safe and well. He referred to the great services of the Royal Air Force during the preparation of the machine, and also during the whole period of flying. Air Vice-Marshal Sir Geoffrey Salmond and his officers were always ready to assist the expedition in every conceivable way. He also expressed indebtedness for the great kindness shown by the Greek Government when the expedition reached Corfu, and for the services rendered by the United States of America and the Imperial Japanese Government in times of great trouble. All Britons would feel that the kind attention of those foreign States showed the existence of a strong friendly feeling between themselves and this country. He proposed the health of Squadron Leader MacLaren and the crew of the Vickers-Napier Vulture.[8]

Mr J. R. Clynes, member of Parliament, in supporting the toast, endorsed the expressions of indebtedness for the services rendered by the other countries whose representatives were seated at that table. He associated himself personally, and as the representative of the government, with the great adventure which had brought them together:

I read in various newspapers, the modest commentaries of MacLaren and his colleagues on this great adventure. There is a true touch of real greatness in the belittling and under-estimating of this mighty enterprise which they undertook. It was, says MacLaren, but a busman's holiday, taken as one would take hold of a bicycle and go on an ordinary journey. We are happy in the possession of that quality of the British character which can undertake adventures involving enormous risks, and yet rate these adventures as ordinary every-day affairs.[9]

Mr Clynes went on to say that in the full development of aviation, the cooperation of governments was not only desirable, it had become essential, and this country had so real an interest in the commercial and trading concerns of its people that our government, whichever party might form it, should not be behind any other government in the world. He thought it would be a blessing for mankind if these tremendous instruments of the air could be devoted solely to civil purposes in order that trade and commerce should be assisted and lines of communications between civilized nations of the world enormously improved. The lands of the earth could be brought still nearer together by the success of great aviators; and, although Squadron Leader MacLaren did not succeed on this occasion, he had the spirit in him that would enable him to make a second effort.

MacLaren, in his address, said:

Mr Chairman, your Excellencies, ladies, wife and gentlemen—I should like, on behalf of my colleagues and myself to express my deep appreciation of the honour you have done us in asking us here today, and to thank the Chairman and Mr Clynes for the very kind words they have spoken about us. As you will realise, it has been a very bitter disappointment to us, as it no doubt has been to everyone, that we should have failed our task, but the sympathy and kindly feelings which all have shown towards us goes far to alleviate it. I am afraid that I was not born to be a speaker, so I hope that you will forgive me if I read out a short resume which I have prepared.

Before I say anything about our own flight, I should like to take this opportunity of offering our warmest congratulations to the American airmen, who within the last few hours have actually succeeded in flying round the world. Their feat is not only without parallel in the history of flying, it is a landmark in human history which will never be forgotten as long as man preserves his sporting instinct and in the true pioneer spirit goes on trying to do something which has never been done before.

We rejoice exceedingly in the success of our American friends, for when our need of a friend was most urgent they proved to be friends indeed. You will remember that our first machine crashed at Akyab in Burma. We were 4,000 miles from our second machine, which was waiting for us at Tokyo. The American flyers had just reached Tokyo, and they immediately resolved on one of the most magnanimous acts of international sportsmanship ever recorded. An American destroyer, which was accompanying their airmen, was detached to take my spare machine all those thousands of miles to Akyab to enable our British effort to be started again.

We had to wait a long time before we could express our thanks in person. We crossed each other in the air between Akyab and Rangoon, and it was not until that second machine had also gone west that we were able to meet face to face at Boston, when the Americans were again on their own soil, after having crossed the Pacific and the Atlantic and the continents of Asia and Europe. And now they have completed their task by crossing their own continent as well.

But the Americans were not the only friends we made on our flight. We went among many nations, and everywhere we were received with the greatest of hospitality, not only by the British communities, but by the people themselves. I should like in particular to mention the warmth of the Italian greeting at Rome, the help the Greeks gave us when we were stranded on a lake in Corfu, the welcome at Athens and by the French in France and Indo-China, and the crowning hospitality of the Japanese. On the soil of the British Empire we lacked nothing needful to make our flight a success. The flight, of course was a purely unofficial one. Nevertheless, we owe a great debt of gratitude to the Royal Air Force. The Air Ministry helped us in every conceivable way, both before and during the flight. They put all their information at my disposal, prepared my maps, and allowed us to make use of their machines and aerodromes.

One of our chief regrets at our failure to complete the Pacific crossing was that we were unable to avail ourselves of the generous preparations which the Royal Canadian Air Force had made for us. Still we enjoyed the active assistance of the Canadian Navy, and but for the gallant little Thiepval, our plight amid the fogs of the Kurile Islands and Kamchatka would have been even worse than it actually was.

And now I should like to say a word about the three firms whose generosity enabled me to organise the flight. It is obvious that the selection of material for an enterprise of this nature entails their most careful consideration and important decisions. I, therefore, took the opportunity of discussing the matter with many experts and the final result was that the combination of Vickers, Napiers and Shell-Mex stood out from any other as giving me my best chance of success. I was indeed fortunate in not having to make any change in this decision through their immediate readiness to co-operate with me in my venture and I do indeed pay this tribute from the bottom of my heart.

Our most grateful thanks are due to Vickers for their wonderful Vulture Amphibians; to Napiers for the splendid engines which carried us across two continents for a total distance of 13,000 miles; and to Shell-Mex for the supply of petrol and oil, which was never found wanting on all our long route. If the flight did not achieve the complete success which we had hoped, it was not the fault of any of these great companies.

The machine was ideal in every way for the venture, the amphibian being undoubtedly the best for the job, and actually saved our lives on more than one occasion, and I cannot sufficiently express my admiration for the way in which she behaved under the most trying and adverse conditions. The engines carried us thousands of miles without causing us the slightest anxiety, and no blame can be attached to them for the unfortunate mishaps at Corfu and Parlu, and the quality of petrol and oil speaks for itself, when I say that not once through the trip did we have to do anything except pour it in the tanks.

We were beaten in the end by fog alone. Vickers, Napiers and Shell not only made our flight possible, but did everything in their power to ensure a successful issue. We give our most cordial thanks.

I would also like to pay tribute to my very gallant companions—Flying Officer Plenderleith and Sergeant Andrews, whose courage and devotion to duty brought us safely through many a trying ordeal. Flying Officer Plenderleith piloted the machine the whole time and never once was his judgement at fault, in spite of the many tight corners we got into. Sgt. Andrews worked incessantly and his pluck and endurance in working on the machine under the most trying conditions was nothing short of marvellous, and many times he refused to give up even though he was unfit to carry on.

I do not know that there is anything very fresh to say about the flight itself. You have probably read in the Press the brief accounts of the different stages which I was enabled to send home through the co-operation of "The Times".

That is our story. We would not have missed the adventure for worlds; we did our best, and failed this time. I will say nothing of our luck; that is all in the game. But I will never say anything disrespectful of a London fog again. It is now established that it is possible to fly round the world. I believe it can be done in less time than Jules Verne's 80 days, and also by one British machine and one British engine. Once more I should like to thank you for the very hearty welcome you have given us, and say that I am very sorry we failed, but we did our best.[10]

There was no doubt that MacLaren, Plenderleith and Andrews, in the face of the huge difficulties faced throughout their attempt to fly round the world, had used their unconquerable determination to continue on and on. This is a wonderful record of human endeavour and endurance.

England may no longer be able to boast the unchallenged supremacy that once was hers in the realm of field sports. But in the power of the scramble to produce the type of man that can confront dangers known and unknown in a brave, adventurous and light-hearted spirit, there is no decline.

On 28 September, the American world flight ended successfully in Seattle, having taken 174 days to cover 27,534 miles in their three Douglas World Cruisers. Showing his respect for their life-saving help on his own journey, MacLaren went to Seattle to welcome them and be present at the completion of their journey.

The crew of the Vulture were never to meet up again. Flying Officer Plenderleith returned to duty, rising to the rank of wing commander, commanding G.R. Squadron. He died whilst on duty in December 1938.

Sergeant Andrews returned to duty after a period of illness and convalescence, rising to rank of warrant officer (fitter 1). He had been presented by the Knaphill Working Men's Club (in Woking, Surrey, where he lived) with an illuminated testimonial as a memento of the gallant effort made by him and his companions during the world flight. He then completed thirty-five years unbroken service before retiring from the RAF in September 1950.[11]

A very thoughtful poem was sent to *The Times* by an anonymous poet:

To MacLaren
    Thine task, though wholly yet undone;
    Ne'er thine heart should repine;
    Great task—'mong millions—attempt one;
    Onward with heart divine,
    To trace the path, that guideth thee,
    Like migratory bird to flee,
    By the wand of Lord shown,
    Facing foul or fair, realm to realm;
    With inward light—thus own –
    "To flight round the world" is thine beam.
    Endurance—must be thine motto;
    And whatever may cast,
    Onward and onward thou shalt go,
    Enraptured with the past:
    Smiling hardships heralding ahead;
    In all the world, no one yet tread,
    Destined thee to fulfil;
    And to one idea thou shalt cling,
    For it is—Lord's Great Will,
    Till real heart and not fancy sing.
    Girdling the globe a great mark,
    For centuries to shine,
    In aerial world, immortal spark,
    Beaming in every clime.
    England, thine England, for her name,
    Thou art fanning the sacred flame;

Though now in shattered hope,
On this dislocated Arakan;
Where to turn, where to grope,
In bewilderment, what to plan?
But yet thine England, dear England,
With glorious eyes austere,
Shall guard thine unfurled banner stand,   M.T.N.
Wherever near and far.   24-5-1924

The Aftermath

MacLaren returned home from Seattle in September 1924 after congratulating the Americans on their success in completing the world flight. This could not have been easy for him, as he saw his own venture as a failure, but had been in respect of the amazing help they had given his crew when the Vulture crashed in Akyab.

He was now returned to full pay by the RAF, as they considered where to enlist him for his next duties. The air force lists note that on 23 October 1924 he was officer commanding Flying Boat Development Flight (FBDF), which was based at Felixstowe in Suffolk. This was an early seaplane station and had been involved in designing and operating some of the first flying boats during the First World War. Now it was renamed the Marine Aircraft Experimental Establishment, and as MacLaren had already spent some time with them in 1923 (before attempting the world flight) under its previous name (Marine and Armament Experimental Establishment), he had the knowledge required to be able to command.

While he was there, he wrote to the Air Ministry asking if he could have an interview with them in connection with 'further proposed activities on my part in the aerial globe trotting line'.[1]

It would seem that he was still full of his adventurous spirit and wanting to achieve that which he had not managed in 1924. Unfortunately, the reply came that there was not much likelihood of being granted permission to make a further attempt at another round-the-world flight at present.

However, MacLaren was once again to be moved on, as Squadron 208, which was stationed in Ismailia in Egypt, was in need of a commanding officer. Having been in the squadron in 1920, it would seem that, with all his experience in Egypt over the past years, he was the right officer for that placement. He was sent out to Egypt on 12 December 1925 and remained with the squadron until 14 March 1927.

During this time 208 Squadron maintained a high standard of training in order to meet its operational commitment, should the opportunity have arisen. They flew RE8s and Bristol Fighters. The highlights which often broke up the training routine during these peacetime years were open days, aerial demonstrations, military searchlight tattoos and even formation escorts for visiting royalty.[2]

The next time that we hear from MacLaren brings very sad news. The reason he returned to England in March 1927 can be found in the letter he wrote from the Officer's Hospital, Royal Air Force, Uxbridge to Sir Hugh Trenchard, now Marshal of the RAF:

Dear Sir Hugh Trenchard,
Very many thanks for the Xmas present to your Godson. It is charming of you to have remembered him, and I know he will be delighted with the toy which I have just forwarded on to him.

You will be sorry to hear that Neuroses has at last overtaken me and that I have had to go to hospital as a result of Gents Rheumatism contracted in Egypt. I was just home on sick leave when the Medical Board collared me, turned me inside out, told me that as a result of this Rheumatism, I have now got disease of the heart and can no longer fly or serve overseas. In other words permanently unfit for posts or otherwise duties, and only fit for home service. Thus, the end of my hopes and ambitions. It is rather a tragedy isn't it?

My very humble congratulations on your promotion, which I read with delight in the papers.

Your Godson is flourishing… and is beginning to talk quite well. His chief interests are engines and aeroplanes, a 'good omen' as a future candidate for the Chief of Air Staff.

My kindest regards to Lady Trenchard and Hugh minor from both Mrs MacLaren and myself.[3]

MacLaren clearly had a close friendship with Hugh Trenchard, as he would have first met him when his family was holidaying in Davos in the early 1900s. Then, having kept in touch throughout his career, MacLaren had asked him to be godfather to his youngest son, Hugh.

It was clear that the extreme weather conditions he had experienced while flying in open-cockpit aeroplanes, so much a part of MacLaren's flying career over the years, had resulted in some dangerous health issues. And after much rest at home with the family in London, he was once again able to return to work. On 9 May 1927 he was moved to Bentley Priory, in Stanmore, Harrow, where he was employed for technical staff duties in control of transport, the Priory having been sold to the RAF the year before to accommodate the Inland Area (Training Command) part of the Air Defence of Great Britain (ADGB).

But by 30 July it became apparent that MacLaren was now unable to maintain any further job in the RAF due to the breakdown of his health, and he wrote once again to Sir Hugh Trenchard to ask if he would give him some form of testimonial to aid him in obtaining employment in civilian life. Having been passed permanently unfit for flying by the medical authorities, including vision problems, it was clear that his career in the RAF was coming to an end.

He approached the Asiatic Petroleum Company, a joint venture between the Shell and Royal Dutch oil companies, and they were willing to interview him. Shell had sponsored him and provided all the fuel for his world flight attempt, so he was well known to them.

In reply, Sir Hugh Trenchard wrote the following testimonial:

Squadron Leader A. S. C. S. MacLaren, O.B.E., M.C., D.F.C., A.F.C., has been an officer in the Royal Air Force and Royal Flying Corps since 1914 and gained considerable distinction during the Great War.

When I knew him some years ago he was useful, energetic, keen and full of initiative.

During 1924 he attempted a very difficult and ambitious flight round the World and managed to cover a considerable portion of the distance. This flight entailed a good deal of early preparation in which Squadron Leader MacLaren showed energy, initiative and some organising ability.

Unfortunately his health has broken down and for some time past it has not been possible to give him the full employment and responsibilities of his rank. This has tended to jeopardise his career in the Royal Air Force and I understand it is on this account that he now wishes to resign.

I trust his health will not prove a disadvantage against him obtaining a post in civilian life compatible with his qualifications and I wish him well.

Marshal of the Royal Air Force

Chief of the Air Staff.[4]

Two other testimonials were also offered to MacLaren in his support. One was from the air vice-marshal, who was commanding Bentley Priory, stating that he was an able and thoroughly reliable officer and a pleasant companion, having carried out his duties in charge of transport to his entire satisfaction. The other came from Air Vice-Marshal Sir Philip Game, who had known MacLaren for the past ten years or so. He wrote that he was a very fine pilot and a good practical mechanic, and that he could thoroughly recommend him for any appointment requiring knowledge of the world, drive and common sense.[5]

In the meantime, MacLaren was clearly in a very bad state, both his physical and emotional health suffering. He and his wife Amanda had moved to many different addresses in London over the years and their three children were growing up. Their eldest son Wallace, aged 11, Anna, aged 9, and her younger brother, Hugh, aged 6, were living with their mother at home. Clearly there were marital difficulties between MacLaren and his wife; it was known that Amanda suffered from severe insomnia, resulting in extreme fits of rage.

They were finally to separate from each other in 1929.

As this occurred, MacLaren was spending some time at RAF Calshot at Southampton Water (where he had begun the round-the-world attempt), an RAF maintenance and training unit that was hosting the Schneider Trophy that year.

However, as late as February 1930, MacLaren was still being considered for a job in the RAF, and he received a letter from the Air Ministry outlining that they had him in mind for a post in the East as aerodrome manager in Hong Kong. The Colonial Office had asked them for recommendations of officers who had good technical experience and were well-versed in air matters.[6]

But unfortunately the breakdown in MacLaren's health and his personal life was to prevent him from considering any further jobs, and on 3 June 1930, *The London Gazette* announced that he was to be placed on the retired list on account of ill health.

This was to be the finish of his career in the RAF.

The Final Days

Following his separation from Amanda and his retirement from the RAF, there was a great deal for Archibald to think about and consider what to do next. He went out to Florence, Italy, taking two of his children, Wallace and Anna, to make contact with his mother, Ethel. He then returned to England, leaving Anna to live with her grandmother for five more years, and taking Wallace back to live with his mother, Amanda, and brother Hugh.

Ethel was liaising with her cousin, Constance Evers, and they were running an International School for Advanced Studies in Arts and Letters called Eversholme, located in La Torre Di Bellosguardo, Florence. These were not easy years for Anna, as all that time she was under the influence of her domineering grandmother.

Although Archibald was only 17 years old when he first met Violet Emily Dimble, it was clear he had never forgotten his love for her. Violet was to explain later in a letter to Archibald's daughter Anna: 'It was a boy's shy love and admiration for a girl of sixteen who was even shyer! There was nothing to tell my mother that what everyone would call a calf love was in reality a lifelong love.'[1]

Archibald had never once written to Violet or attempted to see her when he was married, but after the separation from Amanda he decided to search for her family. He eventually found Violet's mother, Mrs Welford, living in a house called Red Roofs in Rottingdean, Sussex, where she was letting out rooms. Violet had been married to a producer of plays for the BBC, but was now on her own and living with her mother.

Archibald and Violet stayed in Rottingdean with her mother, as there was nowhere else for them to go, and there is no indication that Archibald managed to find any work in civilian life. His health was still steadily deteriorating, and his doctors suggested that it would be better for him to consider going to live where the climate was a little warmer. After they moved to Nice on the French Riviera, his health did recuperate a little. But yet another terrible family tragedy was to bring him great distress.

On leaving Chard School in Somerset, Archibald and Amanda's eldest son, Wallace —no doubt with an introduction from his father—had started an apprenticeship at Messrs. Vickers Aircraft Works in Brooklands, Surrey, where they were manufacturing large aircraft.

However, one day when he was going to work on his motorbike, he collided with another motorcyclist and sustained major injuries to one of his arms, which meant he could no longer continue to carry out his work with Vickers. After this, he acted in an honorary capacity as an assistant master at Burstow School near Horley, Surrey. He was quite a fine artist and loved drawing pictures and sending them to people on postcards and once did a sketch of his father!

As time went by, Wallace's arm was not getting any better, and finally gangrene set in; he was rushed to Southend General Hospital for an emergency operation. Unfortunately, this was not successful, and Wallace died two weeks later on April 17 1938, aged just 20. His funeral and burial took place at St Bartholomew Church at Burstow and in addition to the family mourners, a number of his colleagues from the Vickers works and Burstow School were present.

Archibald's daughter, Anna, had sent a telegram to her father in Nice informing him of Wallace's illness and of course he wanted to return to England as soon as possible to be with his son. But difficulties arose again, which were explained in a letter Violet wrote to Anna in later years:

When your telegram arrived at Nice, telling him of Wallace's illness, he was in a quandary. Trains always made him ill and flying was out of the question and he was recovering from a bad heart attack. He ignored the doctor's advice and started on a nightmare journey back.

> I thought I should never get him home to England. Then the shock of
> the news, and the criticism we had to face over our late arrival undid
> all the good of his time in France.[2]

After Wallace's funeral, Archibald and Violet once again returned to warmer climes, but due to the Italian occupation of the French Riviera at the time, they decided to make another move to Madeira, which had remained neutral during the First World War.

They arrived in Madeira in 1940 and, knowing nothing about the archipelago and having no contacts there, they initially moved into the Atlantic Hotel near Funchal. But gradually Archibald started making connections and became very friendly with the naval control officer in Madeira at the time.

He and Violet were also involved with the Blandy Brothers, who produced the well-known Blandy Madeira wine, and their address in Funchal was often used on the letters which Violet would write home to Archibald's brother Cecil in an attempt to keep him informed of Archibald's steady decline.

Archibald managed almost a year of his health being fairly calm with no further heart attacks, but then things began to go downhill fast. In July 1942, he started being unable to breathe easily and went down with an attack of malaria, a malady that had recurred from time to time over the years. A few days later he suffered a mild stroke and lost sight in his right eye. This was due to a blood clot and the arteries behind the eye were destroyed. Despite medication and help from doctors, he was told on 4 August that his sight would never return and from that time his health seriously deteriorated.

It was also clear that the lower altitude of the town was not making Archibald's breathing any easier, and so he and Violet moved to a small cottage higher up above the sea on the way up to the Monte, which had a cooler climate and more peaceful environment.

Violet nursed Archibald on her own in the months before his death. He started to have bad heart spasms and continued to struggle for breath both day and night, and was naturally terrified of what might happen. But for a whole year, Violet managed to deceive him into thinking that it was all temporary and everybody in Funchal who visited him said that it was she who had kept him alive for his last year.

Archibald died peacefully just after midnight on 18 June 1943, aged 51, and in accordance with the custom of the country was buried in the English Cemetery the following day.

Violet wrote home to his brother Cecil:

Archie was buried in the beautiful little English Cemetery here and a simple and most moving service was conducted by the Rev. Arthur Calderwood M.C., a Scottish padre much loved on the Island.

He gave a moving tribute to Archie's patience and cheerfulness during his long year of suffering and recited those beautiful lines by Rupert Brooke. All members of the British Legion attended and all the people from the Consulate and all the English families so long established here. And the American Consul, a great admirer of Archie, who had been Consul in Shanghai at the time Archie landed there on his world flight and who remembered Archie making a speech. The flowers were of Madeira's best, mostly roses. I have looked after Archie for nearly 14 years and I am left at 50 years of age without the friendship, help and protection of the very nicest man our family have ever met.[3]

An Obituary was placed in *The Times* newspaper on 22 June 1943:

PIONEER FLIER

Sqdn. Ldr. A. S. C. MacLaren, D.F.C., A.F.C., who has died in Madeira, was one of the pioneers of long-distance flights.

In 1918 he piloted a four-engined Handley Page bomber on the first through flight to India.

Five years later he attempted the second round-the-world flight in a Vickers Vulture amphibious biplane, but the venture failed at Kuril Islands, north-east of Japan, 13,000 miles from the starting point.

Sqdn. Ldr. MacLaren was eventually invalided from the RAF. He leaves two children, Mrs. Frank Roach, widow of an RAF pilot, and Mr Archibald Hugh Stuart-MacLaren, at present playing in "The Man Who Came to Dinner" at the Savoy Theatre.

Epilogue

I never knew my grandfather as he died before I was born, but from listening to all the tales that my mother would tell me over the years, discovering many books which mentioned his career as well as meeting the families of his two crew members on the world flight, I began to understand the amazingly adventurous and highly intuitive man that he was.

During his life, it was known that grandfather was always most appreciative of the enthusiasm of his friends and officials, more on behalf of his profession as an aviator and the prestige of British aviation, than for himself for his own personal ability of aggrandisement.

He was always fully aware of the mistakes he made through the years, especially during the world flight. When I received the wonderful gift of the atlas from the gentleman in Scotland, where grandfather had marked out the journey they were to embark on, I discovered one page, at the end of the atlas, where his writing appears and where he clearly understood some of his own mistakes. It reads:

A few home truths <u>not</u> for publication.

What shouldn't have been done (By one who knows)

(1) Machine too heavily loaded (counteracted by fact that Americans were more heavily loaded than we were).

(2) Damned foolishness in trying to cross the Channel in thick fog.

(3) Forced landing at Corfu (fault of engine manufacturers for Swedish steel in their reduction gears, and aircraft

manufacturers for badly designed engine mounting, considering propellor fluttering.

(4) Forced landing at Parlu (exactly the same remarks as above apply to this episode, only intensified 100 times, as most of the later troubles can be traced to this stoppage).

(5) Passed by d'Oisy (strongly commented upon in the papers. Most annoying).

(6) Crash at Akyab. The last and absolute straws that broke the camel's back. Due to the following faults:

a. Under pitched propellor

b. Distorted rigging due to Parlu

c. Waterlogged condition of machine

d. Heavy load (my fault)

e. Fatal mistake of throttling back to land when only flying at stalling speed.

Amen

Corfu]
Parlu]   =   a combination of circumstances unparalleled
Akyab]   in the history of aviation in so far as rotten
                damned bad luck is concerned!!!!
                i.e. This is my own private view of the matter
                and as such should not influence your mind
                on the question.

Finally, in 1993, a newspaper article by Vikki Orvice entitled 'Taking the goggles off the real Biggles' was written to celebrate the centenary of the birth of the best-selling author Captain W. E. Johns, and it discussed likely contenders for the inspiration behind his book *Biggles Flies East*. One of those was definitely thought to be Major Archibald Stuart-MacLaren: 'Just like Biggles, [Major MacLaren's] gun jammed, but instead of shooting him a German pilot waved and flew alongside.'

Archibald Stuart Charles Stuart-MacLaren, my grandfather, will always be remembered in my heart as the most inspiring daredevil that he was.

Appendix

The London Gazette Notices

Appointments and Records of Promotion—*The London Gazette*

War Office—12 July 1915
REGULAR FORCES. SPECIAL RESERVE OF OFFICERS INFANTRY
The undermentioned Cadets and ex-Cadets of the Officers Training Corps. to be Second Lieutenants (on probation): Archibald Stuart Charles MacLaren, 3rd Battalion, Kings Own Scottish Borderers.

25 September 1915
ROYAL FLYING CORPS. *Military Wing*
The undermentioned appointments are made: *Flying Officers*—Second Lieutenant A. S. C. MacLaren, The King's Own Scottish Borderers, Special Reserve, and to be seconded.

27 July 1916
AWARDS TO THE R.F.C.
His Majesty the King has been graciously pleased to confer the Military Cross on the under-mentioned officers in recognition of their gallantry and devotion to duty in the field:
Second Lieutenant A. S. C. MacLaren, K.O. Scot. Bord., Special Reserve, and R.F.C.

9 October 1916
ROYAL FLYING CORPS. *Military Wing*
The undermentioned appointment are made:

Flight Commanders from Flying Officers:
2nd Lt. A. S. C. MacLaren, M.C., K.O. Sco. Bord., Spec. Res., and to be temp. Capt. whilst so empld.

25 November 1916
Temporary Captain A. C. MacLaren relinquishes his commission on account of ill-health, and is granted the honourable rank of Captain.

1 July 1917
K.O. Sco. Bord. A. S. C. MacLaren, M.C., and to remain seconded

6 October 1917
Temp. Capt. A. C. MacLaren relinquishes his commn. on account of ill-health and is granted the hon. rank of Captain.

11 June 1918
ROYAL AIR FORCE—*Air Ministry* FLYING BRANCH
The undermentioned Capts. to be Temp. Majs. while emplyd. as Majs. (A. & S.) –A. S. C. MacLaren, M.C.

5 December 1918
Awards of Foreign Decorations—Royal Air Force
AWARDED Air Force CROSS
Captain (A./Major) Archibald Stuart Charles MacLaren M.C. (EGYPT)

15 May 1919
Memoranda to all officers of the Royal Air Force...
To be acting Majors:
Captain A. S. C. MacLaren M.C., A.F.C., while specially employed

22 December 1919
CENTRAL CHANCERY OF THE ORDERS OF KNIGHTHOOD
St James's Palace, S.W.1.
The KING has been graciously pleased to give orders for the following appointment to the Most Excellent Order of the British Empire (O.B.E.) in recognition of distinguished services rendered during the War:

ROYAL Air Force
Flight Lieutenant Archibald Charles Stuart MacLaren M.C., A.F.C.,

1 April 1920
SPECIAL RESERVE OF OFFICERS—RESERVE UNITS. INFANTRY
The undermentioned Lts. relinquish their commns.
3rd K.O. Sco. Bord.—A. S. C. MacLaren, M.C., and retains the rank
of Lieutenant

14 September 1920
ROYAL AIR FORCE—SHORT SERVICE COMMISSIONS
The following officers are granted short service commissions in the
ranks stated, with effect from the dates indicated, retaining their
seniority in the substantive rank last held by them prior to the grant
of this commission, except where otherwise stated: *Flight Lieutenant*
Archibald Stuart Charles MacLaren O.B.E., M.C., R.F.C.,

4 May 1922
ROYAL AIR FORCE INTELLIGENCE
The following appointments in the Royal Air Force are notified: A. S.
C. MacLaren, O.B.E., M.C., A.F.C., from No. 208 Squadron Middle
East, to command Aden Flight, Middle East 1.4.22

30 June 1922
ROYAL AIR FORCE—*Air Ministry* PROMOTIONS
The undermentioned officers are promoted to the ranks stated—*Flt.
Lts. to be Squadron Leaders* –
Archibald Stuart Charles MACLAREN, O.B.E., M.C., A.F.C.

12 October 1922
ROYAL AIR FORCE INTELLIGENCE—HONOURS
Awards to the RAF in Iraq
The King has been graciously pleased to approve of the following
rewards for distinguished services during active service operations in
Somaliland in March 1922:
D.F.C. - Squadron Leader A. S. C. MacLaren O.B.E., M.C., A.F.C.

20 April 1923
ROYAL AIR FORCE INTELLIGENCE
Appointments: - the following appointments in the Royal Air Force are noted:
Squadron Leader A. S. C. MacLaren O.B.E., M.C., D.F.C., A.F.C., to No 1 School of Technical Training (Boys) Halton, on transfer to Home Establishment

20 November 1923
ROYAL AIR FORCE INTELLIGENCE
Appointments: the following appointments in the RAF are notified:
A. S. C. MacLaren O.B.E., M.C., D.F.C., A.F.C., to Marine and Armament Experimental Establishment, Isle of Grain. 1.12.23

1 June 1930
The undermentioned Squadron Leaders are placed on the retired list on account of ill-health:
Archibald Stuart Charles Stuart MacLaren, O.B.E., M.C., D.F.C., A.F.C.

Endnotes

Chapter 1

1. Nicholas Aldridge, *Time To Spare?—A History of Summer Fields* (Oxford: David Tallboys Publications, 1989), p. 26.
2. Archibald MacLaren, *A System of Physical Education, Theoretical and Practical* (Oxford: The Clarendon Press, 1869).
3. Archibald MacLaren, *The Fairy Family* (London: Macmillan and Co., 1874).
4. Information from the Archivist—Wellington College, Berkshire.
5. Nicholas Aldridge, *Time To Spare?—A History of Summer Fields* (Oxford: David Tallboys Publications, 1989), p.55.
6. Nicholas Aldridge, *Time To Spare?—A History of Summer Fields* (Oxford: David Tallboys Publications, 1989), p.56.
7. Biography from the Tate Gallery website—www.tate.org.uk
8. *The Davos Courier*—Local news and views, *c.* 1930.
9. *The Davos Courier*—Local news and views, *c.* 1930.

Chapter 2

1. MACLARENS (1964)—from the Summer Fields archives
2. Charterhouse School Register 1878—1910.
3. Charterhouse Monitors Register of punishments, July 1908–July 1909.
4. Letter from a master at Charterhouse to John Wallace Hozier Stuart-MacLaren.

5. The National Archives—Army Form B.2075.
6. The Bodleian Library, Oxford.
7. From the Summer Fields archives.

Chapter 3

1. 1911 Census
2. Bradley Court (Agricultural School), Mitcheldean—stock photo - www.alamy.com.
3. Words from Archibald's daughter, Anna Stuart-MacLaren.
4. Hal Giblin and Norman Franks, *The Military Cross to Flying Personnel of Great Britain and the Empire 1914-1919* (Lancing: Savannah Publications, 2008).
5. Nicholas Aldridge, *Time To Spare?—A History of Summer Fields* (Oxford: David Talboys Publications, 1989) p. 57.
6. Aviators' Certificates—www.waterbird.org.uk
7. The Caudron Brothers of Picardy—www.thegoodlifefrance.com.
8. Grace's Guide to British Industrial History—1915 Aviators Certificates UK—www.gracesguide.co.uk.
9. The National Archives, Kew—WO 339/31530.

Chapter 4

1. Michael Napier, *Winged Crusaders* (South Yorkshire: Pen and Sword Aviation 2013) p. 2.
2. *The London Gazette*—25 September 1915.
3. Operations Record Book AIR27/191.
4. Ferdinand Mount, *Kiss Myself Goodbye* (London: Bloomsbury Continuum, 2020).
5. Info and Casualty Form—Active Service (Army Form B.103).
6. Michael Napier, *Winged Crusaders* (South Yorkshire: Pen and Sword Aviation 2013) p.10.
7. Letter from Captain Blackburn, O.C. "C" Flight, 14 Squadron—The National Archives, Kew, 1916.
8. Anne Baker, *From Biplane to Spitfire—The Life of Air Chief Marshal Sir Geoffrey Salmond KCB KCMG DSO* (South Yorkshire: Pen and Sword Aviation, 2020) p. 93.

9. AIR1/689/21/20/14 - The National Archives, Kew.

10. Published in the Calgary Herald, a division of Postmedia Network Inc. July 1924.

11. Published in the Calgary Herald, a division of Postmedia Network Inc. July 1924.

12. Report on Combat in the Air, 13 June 1916.

13. Anne Baker, *From Biplane to Spitfire—The Life of Air Chief Marshal Sir Geoffrey Salmond KCB KCMG DSO* (South Yorkshire: Pen and Sword Aviation, 2020) p.93.

14. Archibald is a boy's name of Spanish origin meaning 'truly brave'.

15. Published in the *Calgary Herald*—a division of Postmedia Network Inc., July 26 1924.

16. *The London Gazette*—25 November 1916.

17. *The London Gazette*—1 December 1916.

18. Army Form A.45.

Chapter 5

1. Caird Publications—*RFC Training School at Aboukir*—www.cairdpublications.com.

2. Caird Publications— *RFC Training School at Aboukir*—www.cairdpublications.com.

3. History of 196 Squadron - https://raf38group.org/196squadron/

4. The National Archives—WO339/31656.

5. Air Force memorandum No. 1.

6. David Jones, *The Time Shrinkers—Africa* (London: Beaumont Aviation Literature, 1977) p. 7.

7. A History of Navigation in the Royal Air Force—RAF Historical Society Seminar at the RAF Museum, Hendon, 21 October 1996.

8. Guy Slater, *My Warrior Sons* (London: Peter Davies Ltd. 1973) p. 183.

9. Report by Brigadier-General A. E. Borton on the journey from England to Egypt.

10. Guy Slater, *My Warrior Sons* (London: Peter Davies Ltd. 1973) p. 183

11. Report by Brigadier-General A.E. Borton on the journey from England to Egypt.

12. Report by Brigadier-General A.E. Borton on the journey from England to Egypt.
13. Guy Slater, *My Warrior Sons* (London: Peter Davies Ltd. 1973) p. 183.
14. Chaz Bower, *Handley Page Bombers of the First World War* (Buckinghamshire: Aston Publications, 1992) p. 39.
15. Royal Air Force Museum—'Casualty form—Officers'.

Chapter 6

1. Guy Slater, *My Warrior Sons* (London: Peter Davis Ltd. 1973) p. 187.
2. Report sent to the General Officer Commanding RAF Middle East—7 October 1918.
3. Letter accompanying MacLaren's report to Chief of Air Staff—14 October 1918.
4. Aeroplane Monthly magazine—December 1978.
5. Sent from Cairo on 7 January 1919 by General McEwan.
6. Christopher Cole and Roderick Grant, *But Not In Anger* (London: Ian Allan Ltd. 1979) p. 34.
7. Report by General McEwan—7 January 1919.
8. Christopher Cole and Roderick Grant, *But Not In Anger* (London: Ian Allan Ltd. 1979) p 36.
9. Criticisms of the V1500 type Handley Page Aeroplane submitted by Major MacLaren.
10. Account of the flight by Group Captain Halley—Aeroplane Monthly (December 1978).

Chapter 7

1. Letter from Major General Salmond to Chief of Air Staff, Air Ministry, 28 August 1918.
2. Instructions for No.1 Aerial Route written by MacLaren - The National Archives, Kew.
3. Three-page letter from MacLaren to all Route Commanders— National Archives, Kew.
4. Instructions for pilots on No. 1 Aerial Route written by MacLaren - The National Archives, Kew.

Chapter 8

1. 216 Squadron Association.
2. *The London Gazette*—22 December 1919.
3. The Daily Express newspaper—13 May 1920.
4. Brigadier Andrew Roe, *Air Power in Somaliland 1920*—Air Power Review Vol 21 No.1- www.raf.mod.uk.
5. Letter from Governor G. F. Archer, Somaliland Protectorate—3 May 1922.

Chapter 9

1. Extract from writings of Charles Andrews *The Flight of the Vulture*.
2. Extract from writings of Charles Andrews, *The Flight of the Vulture*.

Chapter 10

1. Extract from writings of Charles Andrews *The Flight of the Vulture*.
2. MacLaren's own words.
3. Published in the *Calgary Herald*, a division of Postmedia Network Inc. July 1924.
4. Amanda's own words.
5. Extract from writings of Charles Andrews, *The Flight of the Vulture*.
6. *The Times*—from our own correspondent—collected by MacLaren's brother Cecil (no date).
7. *The Times*—Cairo, Thursday, 17 April 1924.
8. Desbleds, L. Blin., 'Flying Round the World? What are its uses?' *(The Sunday Times*, April 20 1924).

Chapter 11

1. *The Times*—from our own correspondent, April 19 1924.
2. extract from writings of Charles Andrews, *The Flight of the Vulture*.

3. Telegram to *The Times*
4. British newspaper report 1924—collected by MacLaren's brother, Cecil.
5. British newspaper report 1924—collected by MacLaren's brother, Cecil.
6. British newspaper report 1924—collected by MacLaren's brother, Cecil.

Chapter 12

1. Extract from writings of Charles Andrews, *The Flight of the Vulture.*

Chapter 13

1. Alexander Frater, *Beyond the Blue Horizon* (London: Picador 2005) p. 254
2. Dispatch from MacLaren dated 27 May 1924 at 1815.
3. *The Times*—from our own correspondent—25 May 1924.
4. Letter to *The Times* from Tokyo, dated 5 July 1924.
5. MacLarens report to *The Times,* 21 June 1924.

Chapter 14

1. *The Times*—from our own correspondent, Hong Kong, July 2 1924.
2. Rudyard Kipling, *The Ryme of the Three Sealers, 1893.*
3. British newspaper report 1924—collected by MacLaren's brother, Cecil.

Chapter 15

1. With thanks to the British Newspaper Archive.
2. *The Daily Express*—Friday, 18 July 1924.
3. British newspaper report 1924—collected by MacLaren's brother, Cecil.
4. Vulture's Log—dated 13 July 1924.
5. *The Times*—22 July 1924.

6. *The New York Times* newspaper report 1924—collected by MacLaren's brother, Cecil.
7. Plenderleith's Log.

Chapter 16

1. Telegram sent to the Air Ministry via the steam trawler HMCS *Thiepval*.
2. American newspaper report 1924—collected by MacLaren's brother, Cecil.
3. Canadian Press Despatch—Vancouver, August 20 1924.
4. British newspaper report 1924—collected by MacLaren's brother, Cecil.
5. MacLaren's speech.
6. *The Times*—Friday, 26 September 1925.
7. *Daily Mail*—letter from John Walton, Upminster.
8. Shell Historical Heritage Archive—The Pipe Line.
9. Extract from writings of Charles Andrews, *The Flight of the Vulture*.
10. MacLaren's speech.
11. Extract from writings of Charles Andrews, *The Flight of the Vulture*.

Chapter 17

1. Letter to Captain T. B. Marson MBE—22 May 1925.
2. Flight Lieutenant D. S. B. Marr RAF—*A History of 208 Squadron*—1966.
3. Personal letter from MacLaren to Sir Hugh Trenchard—undated.
4. Testimonial from Sir Hugh Trenchard—1 August 1928.
5. Testimonial from Air Vice Marshal Sir Philip Game—31 July 1928.
6. Letter to MacLaren from the Air Ministry—5 February 1930.

Chapter 18

1. Letter from Violet Dimble, Madeira, to Anna—1 January 1944.
2. Letter from Violet Dimble, Madeira, to Anna—6 November 1943.
3. Letter from Violet Dimble, Madeira, to Cecil—12 July 1943.

Bibliography

Articles/newspapers

The Davos Courier (Switzerland—editor W. G. Lockett, *c.* 1930)
Canadian Press Dispatch 1924
Charterhouse School Register 1878–1910
Charterhouse School Monitor's Register of punishments: July 1908–
   July 1909
Flight magazine, 27 March 1924
MacLarens (1964)—Summer Fields archives
The Times, 1924

Books

Aldridge, N., *Time to Spare?—A History of Summer Fields* (Oxford:
   David Talboys Publications, 1989)
Allen, P., *The 91 Before Lindbergh* (Shrewsbury: Airlife Publishing
   Ltd., 1984)
Andrews, C. F., and Morgan, E. B., *Vickers Aircraft since 1908*
   (London: Conway Maritime Press Ltd., 1989)
Baker, A., *From Biplane To Spitfire* (Yorkshire: Leo Cooper Ltd., 2003)
Bower, C., *Handley Page Bombers of the First World War*
   (Buckinghamshire: Aston Publications Ltd. 1992)
Boyle, A., *Trenchard* (London: Collins, 1962)
Cole, C., and Grant, R., *But Not In Anger* (Surrey: Ian Allen Ltd,
   1979)

Frater, A., *Beyond the Blue Horizon* (London: Pan Macmillan, 1986)

Giblin, H., and Franks, N., *The Military Cross to Flying Personnel of Great Britain and the Empire 1914–1919: with Service and Biographical Details of Recipients* (London: Savannah Publications, 2008)

Halley, J., *The Squadrons of the Royal Air Force & Commonwealth 1918-1988* (Kent: Air Britain (Historians) Ltd, 1988)

Jackson, R., *The Sky their Frontier* (Shrewsbury: Airlife Publishing Ltd., 1983)

Jones, D., *The Time Shrinkers—Africa* (London: Beaumont Aviation Literature, 1977)

Langham, R., *Bloody Paralyser: The Giant Handley Page Bombers of the First World War* (Gloucestershire: Fonthill Media Ltd., 2016)

London, P., *British Flying Boats* (Gloucestershire: The History Press, 2011)

MacLaren, A., *A System of Physical Education—Theoretical and Practical* (Oxford: The Clarendon Press, 1869)

MacLaren, A., *The Fairy Family—A series of ballads and metrical tales illustrating the fairy mythology of Europe* (London: Macmillan and Co., 1974)

Malinovska, A., and Joslyn, M., *Voices in Flight* (Yorkshire: Pen & Sword Aviation, 2006)

Marr, D., *A History of 208 Squadron* (Anglesey: 208 Squadron Old Comrades Association 1966)

Mount, F., *Kiss Myself Goodbye* (London: Bloomsbury Publishing, 2020)

Napier, M., *Winged Crusaders* (Yorkshire: Pen & Sword Aviation, 2013)

Nesbit, R. C., *The RAF in Camera* (Gloucestershire: Alan Sutton Publishing Ltd., 1995)

Renfrew, B., *Wings of Empire* (Gloucestershire: The History Press, 2015)

Semple, C., *Airway to the East 1918–1920* (Gloucestershire: Pen & Sword Aviation, 2012)

Slater, G., *My Warrior Sons, The Borton Family Diary 1914–1918* (London: Peter Davies Ltd., 1973)

Websites

'1915 Aviators Certificates—UK'—www.gracesguide.co.uk/1915_Aviators_Certificates_-_UK

'Aviators' Certificates ('Ticket or 'Brevet')—www.waterbird.org.uk/seaplane-history-at-windermere/aviators-certificates/

www.cairdpublications.com/scrap/aboukir/aboukir.htm

'The Caudron Brothers of Picardy'—thegoodlifefrance.com/the-history-of-aviation-in-northern-france/

Diana of the Uplands 1903-4 painting by Charles Wellington Furse—www.tate.org.uk

www.greatwarforum.org

'RFC Training School At Aboukir'—www.rafweb.org